ENSLAVEMENT IN Kentucky

MARSHALL MYERS

Published by The History Press
Charleston, SC
www.historypress.com

Copyright © 2022 by Marshall Myers
All rights reserved

First published 2022

ISBN 978-1-5402-5267-8

Library of Congress Control Number: 2022933418

Notice: The information in this book is true and complete to the best of our knowledge. It is offered without guarantee on the part of the author or The History Press. The author and The History Press disclaim all liability in connection with the use of this book.

All rights reserved. No part of this book may be reproduced or transmitted in any form whatsoever without prior written permission from the publisher except in the case of brief quotations embodied in critical articles and reviews.

For Bond.

CONTENTS

Preface   7
Introduction   9

Reading #1.
   Of Lexington, Lewis Robards and the Great Slave Buyout   19

Reading #2.
   In the Civil War, Why Both Sides Wanted Kentucky   25

Reading #3.
   The *Strader v. Graham* Case: Far More Important than It Seems   30

Reading #4.
   The Other Thirteenth Amendment: An Attempt to Avert
      the Civil War   37

Reading #5.
   Kentuckians, the 1850 Fugitive Slave Law and Cass County,
      Michigan   44

Reading #6.
   Bennett Young: The St. Albans Raid and the "Lost Cause"   51

CONTENTS

Reading #7.
  The Berea Incident: The Fear of Slave Owners
    in Madison County   56

Reading #8.
  War Weariness and the Enigma of War   60

Reading #9.
  "My Old Kentucky Home": An Analysis   67

Reading #10.
  Mrs. Keckley's Book and Mrs. Lincoln's Reaction   73

Reading #11.
  General John Palmer: Was He Kentucky's Worst Enemy?   78

Reading #12.
  The Slaughter at Simpsonville: A Massacre Too Long Forgotten?   86

Reading #13.
  The Expulsion at Camp Nelson and the
    Emancipation Proclamation   93

Reading #14.
  If the South Had Won the War   98

Conclusion   103
Bibliography   107
Index   109
About the Author   111

PREFACE

A book is always just the product of one author's mind, a myth that seems to have taken root and made its own place in scholarship. But it is just that: a myth in the minds of the public for centuries and centuries. The truth lies in a series of readers and supporters.

I'm not talking about just having others read the manuscript and comment on its accuracy and its value as a piece of scholarship. Such an action is indeed an immeasurable gift to the writer and—perhaps to other readers too.

Other people often engage in important conversations about the topic of the book and, in turn, become of infinite value to the author. The author has something to share, and those who engage him or her in conversation edge the book's "idea" closer to publication.

Still other important people reckon with the whole of a book, including those who really understand the worth of a publication. Many may hear the author's doubts and frustrations much more realistically than the author—friends, spouses and even lovers. I happen to have a sharp wife. I also must mention my acquisitions editor, Chad Rhoad, who is quite adept at dealing positively with frustration and disappointment. This work I wrote would not have seen daylight without his help. I shall always be indebted to his sage advice and ability to see another more positive side.

But much of the inspiration for this work must go to the late Bernie Willis, the first Black person I ever really knew. I went to a segregated school in Kentucky until I went to high school. In other words, my first eight grades were with Whites alone. In fact, I didn't know about Black people because I had not been around them. I had a limited amount of experience, but in a doctor's office waiting room one day I remember a little Black girl who came with a mean-looking fishhook in her thumb. But because she was Black, she had to wait. Late in my teenage years, as I walked around, I heard the Black folks from the church where they worshipped, and I could make out their singing with great feeling.

A Black sister and brother lived up on the hill across from my place. But I never talked to them, even when he gathered his mail. I had heard Blacks were awful people from all the Whites around our community. Yet I didn't know for sure.

Bernie was, like me, in the school band, and even though he was Black, I struck up a friendship with him. He wanted to know about White people, and I wanted to know about Black people. We were mutually curious about each other. Over the years, we hoped that we understood each other's heritage better. I began to respect him and his world, and although there certainly was some prejudice on both of our parts—probably more on my side—we were better off for being friends.

When I read about slavery even in my own county, I wondered about how I should feel about it. I had heard from Whites that Black people were an inferior race, but I learned from Bernie that, except for his color, he was just like me.

So, this book is a tribute to his race and the tragedy of slavery in Kentucky. It's surely an inadequate payback to Bernie's people, who suffered through very hard times. But early on, slavery became for me no longer an economic question but a moral question. I reasoned that slavery, no matter how it is dressed—and it often assumes various dresses—is a decision between right and wrong effected by some very nice White people, but it still is a matter of morality, not a matter of economics, as many have made it out to be. Throughout this book, we're going to be examining what the people of Kentucky thought about their changing situation, even though the perspective will oftens ound odd to modern ears.

Let these readings guide you as you read about Kentucky's attempt to defend or refute an institution that has little to offer as an explanation other than an economic one.

INTRODUCTION

This book sees slavery in Kentucky from the standpoint of Kentucky citizens who solemnly thought that owning slaves was a right they had as citizens of the Commonwealth. But rather than a long list of generalizations about how slavery developed in the state, slavery's story is told through the eyes of those who experienced it firsthand. For instance, the massacre at Simpsonville particularizes just what guerrilla warfare was like and how it was inflicted on a group of "colored" soldiers on a cattle drive. To be sure, generalizations about history *are* important, but understanding just how it felt to human beings helps to explain why history is so important.

When Kentucky became the fifteenth state in the Union, slavery soon became fundamental to its agriculture-based society. In the Bluegrass Region, large tracts of land were devoted to tobacco and hemp growing. In the western part of the state, farmers grew crops like hemp, corn, wheat and some cotton, calling for forms of labor for which slavery seemed to be the answer.

According to the 1860 federal census, the average slave owner had between four and five slaves. While the large plantations in the Bluegrass and the western portion of the state still had many slaves in various capacities, plantations like those of the lower South were few. In a way, slavery became ingrained in the conservative culture that guarded slavery shamelessly. With an agricultural base, the farmers knew no other way than to keep slaves in order to produce the crops they planted. After all, they saw slavery as a necessity.

Introduction

Kentuckians became so used to slavery in their midst that most Whites saw any chance of abolishing slavery as fruitless. If Kentucky were to make progress economically, Kentuckians had to have slavery, they reasoned. After all, they said to themselves, slavery itself was guaranteed by the federal Constitution. That by itself was quite convincing because, to many Kentuckians, the enslaved were a form of property that could not be legally taken away.

Harold Tallant, in his study of slavery, concluded that most Kentuckians saw slavery as an "evil necessity"; most citizens understood that slavery had to answer some vexing moral questions, but slavery kept the financial engines of the state running smoothly. In fact, the state could not survive economically without slavery, they argued. Any attempt to abolish slavery, then, was met with stiff resistance led by the wealthy slave owners.

But were there that many slaves? There were about 220,000 enslaved people in Kentucky; in other words, one out of four or five people was enslaved. Rather than list all the slave auctions, the Lexington auction serves as a typical example. The city also saw the largest slave auction in the Commonwealth. Learn what a typical slave auction was like in Kentucky in Reading #1.

The state's citizens who were its apologists were willing to use almost any means to fight any attempt by antislavery forces to eliminate slavery. But what about Kentucky made it so alluring to both the Confederacy and the Union? Why did both sides hope against hope to get Kentucky on their side? Understanding the allure of the state to each side is what Reading #2 is about.

Most historians could cite a number of other factors for Kentucky's importance. Kentucky had more slaves than many states, like Texas and Arkansas, states part of the Confederacy. And enthusiastically, Kentucky was dependent on those slaves, it thought, for its existence as a viable economic power. Kentuckians were strong believers in the Constitution. Lincoln, they thought, would stick by the words in such a sacred document as the Constitution. Kentucky, in particular, could keep its slaves—Lincoln would not touch slavery "where it already existed," mainly because the Constitution didn't allow it.

The state then sided with the Union with the pledge of Lincoln and the words of the Constitution that the war was mainly to save the Union. The citizens of the state thought that preserving the Union was a noble enough cause to go to war over and sided with the Union.

Still, there were other reasons why many in the state championed preserving the Union. The political thinking of Senator Henry Clay of Kentucky and his strong belief in the importance of the Union might have also influenced some of the decision makers, for Clay's thinking and his political influence in the state were great.

Cotton, too, was not as central to the agricultural well-being of the state as it was in the Deep South. In essence, Kentucky could not depend on just one cash crop, as much of the South did. The state depended on a variety of crops.

Yet one of the main reasons for aligning with the Union was that Kentucky could keep its slaves, or so it thought. Lincoln said it, and the Constitution guaranteed it, the citizens thought. Either way, the institution of slavery could continue in Kentucky.

It didn't turn out that way, however. The Emancipation Proclamation seemed to turn the war in a new direction. The Civil War became a war, as many in the North now thought, to free *all* the slaves—a direct refutation of Lincoln's pledge and the Constitution's words that said that Kentucky could continue to have slaves. Kentucky was exempted in the Emancipation Proclamation, that was true, but many Kentuckians were not universally convinced that the state's slavery was safe. As a result, its citizens brought out their legal arguments.

Lincoln seemed to be more of an abolitionist than the average Kentuckian could feel comfortable with, it seemed. Fighting for freeing the slaves seemed to be quite possible in the states in rebellion—especially if it was, according to Lincoln, "a war measure," but would freeing all the slaves everywhere be a part of this new emphasis? The result was that Kentucky used almost any method of argument or tactic to keep its slaves, anticipating that the Union would free all slaves everywhere. Consequently, the arguments for and against slavery do not follow any chronological order. They are classified as for or opposing slavery.

Kentuckians could not believe that Lincoln had reversed his stand, even in the end. They could not imagine a culture of the state that would *not* need slavery, as Governor Bramlette said to Lincoln himself when he told Lincoln that his state had been loyal. How could he break a solemn promise? Even after ratification of the Thirteenth Amendment, Bramlette still insisted that the federal government should monetarily compensate Kentucky slave owners. Slavery seemed to be dying a slow death.

In a ruling, the federal Supreme Court, the highest court in the land, used the Graham decision in rendering the Supreme Court's famous Dred Scott decision, a ruling that many people saw as one of the causes of the Civil War and one that affected the institution of slavery within the Commonwealth as well. Reading #3 makes clear its similarities with the famous Dred Scott decision and illustrates the legal arguments the state would make to keep slavery, as pointed out by an article in the *Kentucky Law Journal* by Schwemm.

Later, seeking ratification of the federal government's earlier version of the Thirteenth Amendment was championed by a prominent Madison Countian in the Kentucky legislature. This earlier version also illustrates the legal measures those opposed would use to abolish slavery everywhere. Curtis Burnam and others hoped that the proposed law would convince Kentucky's citizens to rid the country of this highly contentious issue—and avoid a civil war as well. See Reading #4 for an explanation.

While ratification of the first Thirteenth Amendment didn't happen, the earlier amendment became a model to be replaced by a newer version of the Thirteenth Amendment enacted after the war itself.

If President Lincoln was correct in seeing slavery as the "root cause" of the war itself, freeing all the slaves could be an important decision that could have averted that terrible war. It seems obvious that the failed amendment and the acts of the state legislature were just two means to rid the states of slavery.

But legal measures and acts of the state legislature were not the only ways that Kentuckians tried to support slavery. With the passage and strengthening of the Fugitive Slave Law nationally, slave owners thought that if a slave escaped and went to Michigan or any other "free state," he or she had to be lawfully returned to his or her master. Despised by the North, the law made any ordinary White citizens in any state liable by law to return any runaway slaves. Two slave owners from Kentucky tested the Fugitive Slave Law by seeking escaped slaves then in a "free state." The slave owners soon learned that the Fugitive Slave Law's enforcement met with complications they hadn't even imagined. It should be noted that the farmers from Kentucky were operating well within the legal bounds of the Fugitive Slave Law. Read all about this troubling issue in Reading #5.

Bennett Young, a Kentuckian from Louisville, robbed banks in Vermont, assisted by other several other prominent people from his own gang. Although Young said that the robberies, near the Canadian border, were to divert the Yankees in the lower states, he must have thought how grateful the Confederacy would be to receive his plunder. After the war, he did some good in Louisville, but he is best known for being one of the favorite speakers for the "Lost Cause" movement in the South, a way to minimize the role slavery had and divert attention away from the root cause of the war.

By late 1864, the aim of the war was clearly on freeing the slaves, and Kentucky was appalled. The people in the North and Lincoln himself were tired of war and looking for ways to end it. The nation had been too long at war, and the war itself was not going well, with Lee and his army piling up victory after victory for the Confederacy. If something didn't change, the voting public would see change as the only option. The public wanted compromise with the South, and slavery in Kentucky became a much-discussed topic. Read about those trying times in Reading #6.

It is difficult to measure how much influence the abolitionists had on the citizenry of the state. Their persuasion and influence may have been considerable since the slave owners from southern Madison County went so far as to tell several White families (supposedly with antislavery leanings) to vacate the state. The reason these slave owners gave was that they were afraid of reprisals from abolitionists in the rest of the county. See Reading #7 for that.

Although most enslaved people in the state tried very hard to avoid forcing their masters to make financial decisions that involved them, they knew that a master's indebtedness could force him to sell his or her slaves to pay off the debts. These same slaves realized what fates would befall them if they were "sold South" to pick cotton on hot, endless days of work in unforgiving sun. In their minds, being sold was a dreadful move to be avoided at all cost.

The composer Stephen Foster, in the words of the state song, "My Old Kentucky Home," captured the minds of slaves worried about being sold and leaving their homes in Kentucky, where slavery was, according to them and some historians, much "milder." Reading #8 takes a closer look at this classic tune that tries to capture the feelings of the enslaved people who lived on their plantation. The slaves knew that if "hard times come a-knockin'," they would be sold South to the dreaded cotton patches, where the work was drudgery and largely unrewarding.

But the market for slaves was much better in the Deep South. Rumors that Kentucky had "slave farms" that bred only the finest and strongest of slaves were tall tales that fueled a supposed market and worked in the slave owners' favor. Such a market, in fact, prompted many slave owners to sell their excess slaves at the highest price, even considering that he or she might be breaking up a slave family.

Kentucky reached a point in the 1840s and 1850s where it had too many slaves. In a twist of fate, the law of supply and demand meant that slave owners could make handsome profits by selling slaves "down south." Money and opportunity invited slave owners to sell their excess slaves for great profits.

Introduction

But despite all the legal wrangling and the Fugitive Slave Law, the "irresistible conflict" was just that, and the war came. But slaves in Kentucky saw the chance to earn their freedom. After all, hadn't the Emancipation Proclamation freed the Southern slaves in the states of rebellion? Later Lincoln broadened this to include even Kentucky ex-slaves to give them the opportunity to actually fight for their own precious freedom. Thousands of "colored" soldiers and later their families flocked to recruiting stations, like Camp Nelson near Nicholasville, to join in the fight for their freedom.

Slaves were encouraged by what "Massa Linkum" said and did. Even though she had grown up with slaves in Lexington, Kentucky, Mary Todd Lincoln, the president's wife, had an ex-slave as a confidante. Although she was employed as a dressmaker, Elizabeth Keckley did indeed share secrets with the first lady. Slaves thought that this was a harbinger of things to come. Such a close relationship gave hope to the former slaves that freedom meant much to the Lincoln family and that equality was in the near future. Keckley quickly became a role model for the enslaved. Reading #9 looks at the troubled relationship between Elizabeth Keckley and Mary Todd Lincoln—after all, Mrs. Keckley was a former slave.

Yet the slaves, many congregating in Louisville, still needed a White man to sanction their quest for freedom for Black men, women and children. They soon learned that General John Palmer, the military governor over all of Kentucky, including Louisville, was handing out passes (mockingly called "Palmer passes") that gave enslaved people permission to go wherever they wanted. Palmer, himself an antislavery military man, seemed intent to free as many slaves as possible. The White slave owners who desperately depended on slaves to harvest crops soon loudly voiced their displeasure at Palmer's actions. He had "ruined" Kentucky agriculture, they said. Palmer's story is quite interesting, not only for his bravery but also for his commitment to an almost single purpose. Reading #10 covers many of Palmer's actions.

In spite of Palmer's actions, the Kentucky countryside was filled with guerrillas, usually ex-soldiers from the Confederate army who "free-lanced" by stealing, intimidating and murdering ordinary citizens in Kentucky small towns. These guerrillas had been the bane of several military governors like Union General Stephen Gano Burbridge, whose methods of handling these guerrillas was highly unpopular with many Kentucky citizens, who called him "Butcher Burbridge." Burbridge's extremely harsh tactics backfired, as many Kentuckians aided and abetted the guerrillas.

A massacre began when a group of "colored" soldiers was driving a herd of cattle to Camp Nelson in a cold rain near Simpsonville; they were attacked

Introduction

by a group of Confederate guerrillas, who killed every hapless member of this group of soldiers, whose powder was wet, making it difficult to respond.

Some Kentuckians saw the guerrillas' motivation as simply the presence of "colored" soldiers themselves. After all, they were all ex-slaves; many Kentuckians agreed that formerly enslaved had no business "parading" as legitimate soldiers. The guerrillas skulking at Simpsonville saw red and attacked. Reading #11 details the events in the massacre.

But Black residents gained much sympathy after tragedy struck at Camp Nelson. A group of two hundred women and children were expelled from the camp one cold and rainy November day. The women, who were living near the camp, had supported themselves by cooking and ironing for the Black soldiers at the camp. More than two hundred of them were made, in the eyes of many, the victims of the worst kind of racial prejudice, a cruelty indefensible. One hundred of the women and children died of exposure. The gory details are covered in Reading #12.

The incident put an ugly face on the military's prejudice and gave the general public pictures of real women and children suffering; the press asked some rather embarrassing questions about the treatment of former slaves. Slavery again was back in the news.

By contrast, by this time, many Kentuckians were wondering why the state had stuck with the Union. It had provided the number of soldiers asked for and had done all the things the federal government asked, but it was treated unfairly. Governor Thomas Bramlette reminded Lincoln that Kentucky was being treated as a seceded state. The several slights Kentuckians had to endure from the federal government stuck in the craws of many residents.

Even though the cause of eliminating slavery was a noble goal, Kentuckians turned their support and sentiment south, ignoring any attempts to deal with slavery. After a series of governors who were ex-Confederate veterans, Kentucky embraced values that more distinctly aligned them with those states that seceded rather than side with its Northern neighbors, but the state farmers were convinced that agriculture was less possible without slaves. Reading #13 has the details.

The state slowly slipped into a postwar economic rut, and even though it suffered from the loss of its slaves, it most closely identified with its neighbors to the south. One historian later quipped that Kentucky "joined the Confederacy after the War." Why and how it reached that point are fascinating.

According to the federal national citizen test, the exam that all non-citizens must take, in the section on history, a question asks, "What is the cause of the Civil War?" This test accepts two answers as correct: slavery and states' rights. In other words, either answer is considered the right choice. But are there other causes or events that led to the Civil War? Is "states' rights" just a cover for the real reason of freeing the slaves?

To answer the question, what would so sow the seeds of discontent that a nation would go to war with itself? For example, one source lists thirteen events, movements, people or ways of thinking as causes of the war, like states' rights, the Missouri Compromise, the Dred Scott decision, the abolitionist movement, Harriet Tubman, the Underground Railroad, Harriet Beecher Stowe's *Uncle Tom's Cabin*, secessionism and Lincoln's election as president of the United States. According to this list and other sources, each of these factors helped bring on the conflict. To discuss the "appropriateness and validity" of each one would take more space than is available.

All told, 618,000 people died in combat or from disease during the war: 380,000 from the Union and 258,000 from the Confederacy. (It should be noted many more died from disease than from combat.) These are figures that must be marked as uncertain, since we really don't know the true figures; such numbers are the best estimates we have.

The death toll in the Civil War represents by far the most Americans who have died in any war in our nation's history. Could that be one of the reasons why the war stands out? Could it be that one of these reasons is a root cause for all the others? In his second inaugural address, Abraham Lincoln singled out "slavery" as the cause of the war. He said, "All knew that this interest was, somehow, the cause of the war." Kentucky was unusual. It fought for the Union with the promise that it could keep its slaves, because Lincoln said he would not destroy slavery where it already existed and the Constitution would not allow it. In Lincoln's own words, he said, "I have no purpose, directly or indirectly, to interfere with the institution of slavery in the States where it exists. I believe I have no lawful right to do so, and I have no inclination to do so." Kentuckians took Lincoln at his word.

Yet when slavery was outlawed in Kentucky and elsewhere, Lincoln's popularity in the state plummeted. But Lincoln remained steadfast, and the history of slavery in Kentucky saw slave owners asking for compensation for each slave, but compensation never came; most Kentucky slave owners were left with seething anger and resentment—a reason that Kentucky turned Southern.

Reading #14 speculates on the history of slavery in the Commonwealth if, as many had predicted, the South had won the war—a distinct possibility, according to many historians. The North did have greater numbers and stronger industry, employing many people. The South's economy was more agricultural. While Lincoln appointed general after general, only to see them fail in the field, Union General U.S. Grant resorted to attrition, reckoning that he could always resupply men for battle from the almost endless supply of Union soldiers, while the Confederacy couldn't. Such tactics resulted in victories but also bloodbaths, like at Cold Harbor. Lincoln was pleased that at least Grant would fight and generally supported the tactics used.

As Lowell Harrison noted, one of the main casualties of the war was the loss of slavery in the Commonwealth. Many stories circulated that slavery was not dead in the state. A number of slave owners continued the practice after the Thirteenth Amendment was ratified. But the institution of slavery was dead. What Kentucky thought was a sure thing turned out to not be true, and it lost its slaves.

Maybe the loss of slavery is the reason the Thirteenth Amendment was not ratified by the state legislature until 1976.

READING #1

OF LEXINGTON, LEWIS ROBARDS AND THE GREAT SLAVE BUYOUT

In a senatorial debate with Judge Stephen Douglas in Peoria, Illinois, in October 1854, then candidate Abraham Lincoln described the contemporary notion of a "slave trader":

> [A] *sneaking individual of the class of native tyrant, known as the "Slave Dealer." He watches your necessities and crawls up to buy your slave at a speculative price. If you cannot help it, you sell to him; but if you can help it, you drive him from your door. You utterly despise him. You do not recognize him as your friend or even as an honest man. Your children must not play with his; they may frolic freely with little negroes, but not with the slave dealer's children.*

But Lincoln was not the only individual who heaped such opprobrium on the slave dealer. Another contemporary said, while limiting his authority, "I am no prophet. Negro traders are the greatest curse of our land, and I do wish the city council would impose such a tax as to drive them from our midst." In his history of slavery in Kentucky, even in other parts of the Commonwealth, Marion Lucas described slave dealers as "the most publicly despised individuals in Kentucky." Yet these descriptions require careful delineation.

The War Wearied Lincoln Terribly.
Courtesy of Library of Congress.

An Alternative Picture

In Lexington, Kentucky, during the 1850s, things were quite different. Money reigned, and slave traders were just ordinary businessmen in the center of slave trading, particularly at "Cheapside," where the enslaved were regularly and vigorously sold on the auction block. Several factors led to the increased sale of slaves in Kentucky and made Lexington the center for slave sales in the Bluegrass Region—and, indeed, one of the most active in the entire nation.

One factor favoring Lexington was that markets like Louisville and Maysville were too close to the Ohio River, tempting slaves to escape to freedom. Thus, if a slave owner lost just one slave, he or she was out a substantial amount of money.

Another factor was that the Bluegrass Region had the largest number of slaves in the state because the topography of the region favored large hemp and tobacco farms. Such numbers of slaves were well beyond what the farmer needed.

Still another factor was that by the early part of the nineteenth century, Kentucky had an excess number of slaves. Slavery was "needed" when planters and farmers "needed" to clear land and sow fields in the early days of the state. But even when the slave owners ran cattle and grew tobacco and hemp, Kentucky still had fewer claims for slaves since few plantations existed and required a large number of slaves.

Slave Owners Draw Up One Plan

To reduce excess numbers of slaves, slaveholders decided that they would sell as many slaves as necessary. After all, slaves were costly to keep, with clothing, food and other items eating up the slave owners' profits.

Two key events happened that fueled the need for slaves in the lower South. First, the War of 1812 opened up vast territories in the Deep South to settlement—places like Mississippi, Alabama and parts of Louisiana where the soil was rich and would support cotton, rice and sugar cane farming. In fact, these areas needed even more slaves after Eli Whitney's cotton gin perfected the "de-seeding" of cotton and made the plantation system highly lucrative.

Important, too, was that the open land was quite suited for large plantations that could grow many acres of cotton, rice and sugar cane—all crops that required many more slaves than those "extras" in Kentucky.

Secondly, Kentucky did indeed have extra slaves, especially after the law preventing slave importation was reversed in 1849. But in spite of the new law that no longer forbad the selling of slaves from other states and places, Kentucky had enough "extra" slaves that it could possibly meet the lower South's need for them.

While Kentucky grew crops like hemp, the state did not need the large number of slaves for that or any crop, including herding livestock and crude farming. To look at it another way, the state did not produce a large amount of any merchandisable crop that demanded a large number of slaves. The average slave owner in Kentucky had only between five and six slaves—not the large numbers of slaves needed in the Deep South, but the slave owners welcomed an opportunity to reduce the "unnecessary" slaves they had in their possession.

The slave owners from Kentucky thought that they could use their flatboats on the Ohio and Mississippi Rivers to inexpensively transport enough of their "extra slaves" to the plantations of the lower South. Estimates as to the number of slaves transported and sold this way vary considerably. One Kentuckian counted fourteen flatboats loaded with slaves cruising down to the Deep South. The largest slave owner in the 1840s in Fayette County, "Old Duke" Robert Wickliffe, estimated that six thousand slaves left the Bluegrass for the Deep South each year. Estimates varied since there was no formal way to keep track of the numbers.

Slave Owners Turn to Slave Traders

Soon the slave owners looked to the "slave traders" (those who acted as middlemen) in Lexington for guidance and convenience. Rather than use flatboats to transport their excessive numbers of slaves and make the long journey downriver to Natchez, Mississippi, and other places, the slave owners turned to the professionals of slave trading.

But these slave traders in Lexington were not as hated as they were in other parts of country. In fact, slave traders in Lexington and the immediate area during this time were seen as respectable businessmen; just like livestock traders, they were seen as performing a necessary service for the community and local economy.

Lewis Robards Dominates the Slave Traders

One of the first to advertise his services as a slave trader was Lewis Robards, available then at the Phoenix Hotel; he would pay for "likely" slaves at "Premium Prices." Soon other traders followed suit and solicited for "likely" slaves, too, at local hotels in the Bluegrass Region. But Robards was particularly successful at his business, and his slave trading soon netted him a great deal of money. Yet at the end of the boom in sales, the slave traders did not become wealthy citizens. Neither Robards nor other traders became exceedingly rich from their slave trading business—too much overhead and too many lawsuits, and illegal sales offset the profits the various slave traders made. But during the "boom," the slave traders made money.

In fact, Robards, called the "prince of slave traders," was at one time doing so well that he rented Pullum Jail in Lexington and the Lexington Theatre downtown, remodeling them to suit his and other slave traders' purposes. One floor of the Pullum Jail soon became home to his "fancy girls," while a second area was set aside for slave pens, "jailing" the slaves he and other traders were planning on selling later in the Deep South.

The old theater was also used exclusively for his disease-infested slave pens, all the time readying the occupants for sale down south. Robards bragged that the remodeled theater building was "the largest and best constructed for a jail in the West." Orville Browning, a friend of Lincoln's and a native Kentuckian, happened to be in Lexington in 1854 and was invited to see the slaves and the "wares" of the "fancy girls":

> *After dinner* [I] *visited a negro jail—a very large brick building with all the conveniences of comfortable life, including hospital. 'Tis a place where negroes are kept for sale—Outer doors & windows all protected with iron gates, but inside the* [apartments] *are not only comfortable, but in many respects luxurious. Many of the rooms are carpeted & furnished & very neat, and the inmates whilst here are treated with great indulgence & humanity, but I must confess it impressed me with the idea of decorating the ox for the sacrifice. In several of the rooms, I found very handsome mulatto women, of fine persons and easy genteel manners, sitting at their needle work awaiting a purchaser. The proprietor made them get up & turn around to show advantage their finely developed & graceful forms—and the slaves were this I confess rather shocked at my gallantry. I required the price of one girl which was $1600.*

Obviously, Browning saw the "home" of the "fancy girls" as less than humane treatment, a view he quickly relayed to his friend Lincoln. Browning's remark about the "girls" as "decorating the ox for the sacrifice" is revealing.

Robards Worked Legally and Illegally

Louis Robards was a businessman intent on making money almost any way he could—legally or illegally. Legally, he accumulated money and land buying human flesh in a market when the demand for slaves to sell south was so lucrative.

Although not caught acquiring slaves illegally, Robards was often accused of selling infirm or sick slaves too ill to perform work. In addition, Robards paid men to "kidnap" slaves who happened to be "available" to be captured, with little or no regard for the slave owner.

For example, Robards customer David Smith of Garrard County bought a slave woman named Isva who shortly showed violent signs of some illness, including a "shortness of breath." Smith filed suit against Robards, who knowingly sold the sick woman. Smith hoped to at least get his money back. But Robards, caught in a typical practice of selling ill slaves, weaseled out of paying a large fine using his usual courtroom tactics and deferment, which had worked so many times before.

Robards, in turn, was known to turn several "less shady" deals, including using black shoe polish to hide scars and deformities that would affect the price of slaves.

Lexington Is Flooded with Slave Traders

There were other slave traders in Lexington and the surrounding area also in business for a quick buck. In fact, one resident concluded that there "were as many slave traders as there were mule traders!" The list is extensive and includes names like Bolton, Dickens, Thompson, Blackwell, Murphy, Colwell, Brent and Lucas; Lewis Robards's brother, Beck Robards, among many others, quickly got into the slave trading business while the demand for slaves in the Deep South was so strong. After all, to these men, big money was to be made.

Auctions Held at "Cheapside"

Most of the auctions of enslaved people were held at "Cheapside" in Lexington (the name did not indicate that prices were low), as sales of human flesh became so popular and the demand for slaves reached a fever pitch. But the markets for "fancy girls," for instance, were in Lexington and New Orleans. To many in the South at this time, however, Lexington, Kentucky, was the best place to buy slaves generally because of the selection. To those buying in the Deep South, the Bluegrass Region was flooded with an excess number of slaves.

Soon those numbers diminished rapidly, as the market in Lexington shrank. The supply couldn't meet the demand.

This period in Lexington's history is not a chapter that bears repeating. Fortunately, slavery and the inhumane treatment of human beings are nearly dead. Winston Coleman's book *Slavery Times in Kentucky* admonishes historians that "the sale of every slave was not tinged with the chicanery or sharp practice. In the end, the dealers came to symbolize the shame and brutality of an institution which would be washed away only in the blood and tears of a terrible Civil War."

READING #2

IN THE CIVIL WAR, WHY BOTH SIDES WANTED KENTUCKY

Any study of Kentucky and the Civil War usually includes President Abraham Lincoln's explanation of why he thought keeping Kentucky in the Union was an absolute necessity: "I think to lose Kentucky is nearly to lose the whole game. Kentucky gone, and we cannot hold Missouri, nor, as I think, Maryland. These all against us, and the job on our hands is too large for us."

Jefferson Davis, the president of the Confederacy, thought that having Kentucky was just as important to the South's cause, too. In an impassioned letter to Kentucky governor Beriah Magoffin, Davis assured the Kentucky governor that the Confederacy intended to keep its hands off the Commonwealth and respect Kentucky's neutrality in the early days of the war, hoping that such restraint would later steer Kentucky toward the Confederate cause. In the same letter, Davis vigorously objected to the occupation of Union forces at Camp Dick Robinson in Garrard County and to the distribution of "Lincoln guns," designed to aid Union supporters in the central portion of the state.

But Kentucky worked hard to achieve neutrality and strived to mediate between the North and South to avoid the internecine war, but neutrality seemed short-lived when the Confederates occupied Columbus in far western Kentucky and angered the Union-leaning state legislature, which quickly aligned itself with the Union.

The South saw the stationing of troops at Camp Dick Robinson as a clear violation of the neutrality that most Kentuckians sought at the time and a justifiable reason to seize Columbus—vital, they thought, to control of the Ohio and Mississippi Rivers.

Yet as clear as these Northern and Southern violations were, the North and South each still truly wanted Kentucky to fight for its cause. Why? What was there about the state that was so alluring to both the North and South? Union supporters and others pointed out the most obvious reason: the natural defensive border that the seven hundred miles of the Ohio and Mississippi Rivers formed—a natural line Confederate forces could occupy in defense of any Yankee incursion into the lower South.

But Kentucky sided with the North, and the Ohio and Mississippi Rivers were not the natural defense line the Confederates wanted. As a result, the state was not the scene of numerous battles and rampant destruction. With the exception of the Battle of Perryville within the state, the battles were few and limited, unlike for states on the border of the Confederacy. Instead, in Kentucky, skirmishes were the rule rather than large pitched battles with seas of blue and gray. Most battles of real consequence in the geographical area occurred south of Kentucky in Tennessee.

Lowell Harrison's book on the Civil War lists a number of political and economic factors that made the Bluegrass State so inviting to both the North and the South. Kentucky was ninth in population in the country. With that many people, Kentucky was an economic power to deal with.

In agriculture—and in a largely agricultural nation, no less—Kentucky harvested a variety of crops, including hemp, flax, corn and wheat. Some of the grains were ingredients in bourbon whiskey, then as now identified with the Commonwealth. Kentucky also produced many hands of tobacco, often shipped by river to destinations north and south. Overall, in the value of farms, Kentucky ranked seventh in the nation, while coming in at fifth place in the overall value of its livestock. Adding to those figures, even in these early days of the republic, Kentucky was already well known for its horses and mules. In fact, Senator Henry Clay's attempts at raising excellent horseflesh helped plant the seed for the state's development of choice horse farms known today as an important segment of the horse industry.

But vastly important in the minds of mid-nineteenth-century Kentuckians was the question of slavery. In fact, all the states that seceded from the Union were slave states. Seceded states like Arkansas and Texas even had fewer slaves than Kentucky, so many Kentuckians saw the existence of slavery as central to the question of secession. To be more particular, according to Harold Tallant, Kentuckians saw slavery as an "evil necessity" for the overall economy of the state. Most Kentuckians believed that the federal government had no business interfering with slavery in the Commonwealth, as most Kentuckians believed that the federal Constitution guaranteed slavery.

As a result, many Kentuckians concluded that the state should join its Southern brothers in what Vice President of the Confederacy Alexander Stephens called a "slavocracy." Lincoln's "House Divided" speech was then a clear indication that Lincoln meant to end slavery in the *entire* nation, including Kentucky.

Curiously, though, a vast majority were willing to stay in the Union if Lincoln would allow slavery to exist. The issue of slavery in Kentucky, however, is a complicated one involving matters of kin and other genteel relationships.

There are, then, more familial, sentimental reasons that both sides wanted Kentucky in their folds. Its citizens had strong ties to both sides. In fact, much of the Deep South was settled by Kentuckians, who became the early founders of Alabama, Mississippi, Texas and Arkansas. Thus, the culture was similar to the Bluegrass State's. In fact, the president of the Confederate States of America, Jefferson Davis, was actually born in Kentucky and proud of his Kentucky roots.

The dialects of many Southerners, even today, have roots in the dialects of those in Kentucky. "Speaking my language" meant much to these early settlers of much of the South. While many patricians spoke in a different dialect, the vast majority of White citizens, the so-called common people, reflected the broad and deep influences of their Kentucky ancestors.

At the same time, many of the early pioneers of Kentucky later left the state for the lower quarters of Ohio, Indiana and Illinois—some to escape the horrors and competition of slavery and others, like the president's father, Thomas Lincoln, to get a "clear title." Even Daniel Boone, known for opening up Kentucky to settlement, had trouble getting a clear title to his land, with many land companies granting ownership to the same land. The land itself above the Ohio and Mississippi Rivers was rich in soil and the economic opportunities for advancement in states where upward mobility was indeed possible without the stain of slavery. For whatever the reason, many settlers of these states in the lower Midwest had Kentucky roots in culture and heritage. While they were not generally ardent abolitionists, the pull to remain in the Union was strong in these Midwest neighbors.

The dialects in those parts of Ohio, Indiana and Illinois also shared similar form of speech. While the patricians of the Deep South were not included in this, the common people of Kentucky were well represented.

Even today, crossing the Ohio and Mississippi Rivers does not mean that travelers confront a radically different dialect.

Prior to the opening of railroads, the two rivers were the main arteries of commerce in the region for much of the South and, at the same time, the Midwest. Flatboats filled with produce from the East and much of the Midwest and South became familiar sights on the rivers. Abraham Lincoln, as a youth, like many others, made the long river journey from southern Indiana to ship goods to New Orleans.

Because of the falls at Louisville, then, the Derby City became quite important for commerce on the Ohio River east of the city. The river town quickly became the meeting place for traders from the North and the South. At the same time, Louisville also became a center of trade in slaves who had been "sold South" on their way to plantations in the cotton-growing region. Those arguing for secession made their case that the market for selling excess numbers of slaves would close if Kentucky backed the North. The city, in fact, had become infamous at the time for the vigorous trade in slaves, a city filled with slave pens where slaves were kept until their sale.

Sometimes, though, runaway slaves often used the Ohio River as a "Jordan," where they could cross over to freedom in Indiana on their way, many times, to become integrated into Canadian society. The river town quickly became the meeting place for those from both the North and the South.

Quite alluring, too, was that Kentucky, during these early days of the republic, had long been important for its political leaders. The most famous, for his attempts to avoid the specter of war, was Henry Clay, whose Compromises of 1820 and 1850 at least delayed the Civil War. After Clay's death in the years before the war, Senator John J. Crittenden assumed Clay's mantle of compromise and proposed his own valiant attempt at avoiding the war. Although he worked tirelessly to prevent the "irrepressible conflict," both sides summarily rejected his proposal in spite of his political persuasion.

Yet Kentucky's political power still was firmly felt in the election of 1860, as candidates John C. Breckinridge, Abraham Lincoln and even the already mentioned Jefferson Davis were all born in Kentucky. In the election, Kentucky residents were often confused and pulled in different directions, unable to unite around one candidate. But in the end, the Constitutional Union Party of John C. Bell—who proposed compromise, slavery and staying in the Union—won the state. And for the duration of the war, Kentucky *did* align itself, sometimes very reluctantly, with the Union, but the Commonwealth did keep its slaves. Neutrality had not worked, and violence tore at the fabric of the Commonwealth as it settled into an uneasy peace.

But the bottom line is slavery, as the South wouldn't have been interested in Kentucky nearly as much as it was. Slavery in Kentucky was well established; it was already a part of the culture. But Kentucky had too many slaves—more than ever before. It wanted to get rid of a few.

READING #3

THE *STRADER V. GRAHAM* CASE

FAR MORE IMPORTANT THAN IT SEEMS

Background

Who could have known that a legal decision would be a major factor in starting the Civil War? As might be expected, lawyers and judges consistently wrangled over the slavery question in the nineteenth century, as parties north and south wanted the Supreme Court to decide on matters that involved slavery. A case from Kentucky, in particular, involved a slave owner and two runaway slaves that seemed, as far as slave owners were concerned, to answer a vital question about slavery.

But in 1856, instead, the same case provided a precedent for one of the most important Supreme Court decision in the nation's history. In fact, one legal scholar noted that the decision may be the most important decision ever handed down by the U.S. Supreme Court.

The Dred Scott Decision

Many historians argue that the 1856 Dred Scott ruling was a major cause of the Civil War.

The 1856 Dred Scott decision stated that African Americans were not and never could be citizens. In fact, they had no rights like those of White citizens at all because, in the court's view, even if they were born in this country, they weren't citizens. Additionally, the Supreme Court ruled that

Guerrilla Warfare Wasn't Fair. *Courtesy of Library of Congress.*

the Missouri Compromise, largely the work of Kentuckian Henry Clay, was unconstitutional. That agreement had led to the admission of Missouri as a slave state and Maine as a free state. Clay, dubbed the "Great Compromiser," was convinced that the agreement he worked out was a way to keep the delicate balance between slave states and free ones and kept war in abeyance. So, in many ways, the compromise seemed to satisfy both sides and delay any internecine conflict. But the famous Dred Scott decision of 1856 from the highest court in the land opened a wound so cancerous that it took a civil war to excise it from the body politic.

Writing for the majority, Chief Justice Roger B. Taney, from Maryland, a slaveholding state, maintained that the federal government had no right to declare slavery unconstitutional in the various territories and ruled that having slavery was not grounds for admitting or refusing a territory admission to the Union.

The Dred Scott decision was, indeed, a blockbuster. To the opponents of slavery, it was a bitter pill to swallow. To southerners, it seemed to validate what the South was saying about slavery and negate all that the North was espousing about the "peculiar institution." Noted present-day

Constitutional scholar Carl Brent Swisher calls the Dred Scott decision a ruling that "achieved the greatest notoriety and had the greatest effect upon the course of events."

THE *STRADER V. GRAHAM* DECISION

But we should not get ahead of ourselves. In 1851, the Kentucky case *Strader v. Graham*, ultimately decided by the Supreme Court, provided an important precedent for the Dred Scott decision.

Carl Brent Swisher maintains that "the principle [of the *Strader v. Graham* case] was an important one, and prevented a great deal of strife had the [Supreme] Court adhered to it in the famous Dred Scott case decided six years later."

Swisher is not advocating that slavery was acceptable. He notes that the Dred Scott decision was far too sweeping in its ruling and excited too much unnecessary strife. The intent in the Supreme Court in the *Strader v. Graham* case five years earlier was to clarify just how slavery was to be dealt with in a particular but important situation.

In other words, the U.S. Supreme Court extrapolated from *Strader v. Graham* to make its Dred Scott ruling, but Dred Scott went too far. The facts of the earlier 1851 *Strader v. Graham* case seemed simple enough. Graham owned two slaves, Henry and Reuben, who were under the guidance of George Williams, a free man of color. Henry and Rueben were to play at musical concerts in Ohio, Indiana and southern Illinois to drum up business for Graham Springs.

THE GRAHAM SPRINGS RESORT

Graham, in fact, was the owner of Graham Springs, one of the most famous "watering places" in the area. In the first part of the nineteenth century, "watering places" referred to spas that existed throughout Kentucky where the upper crust of the aristocracy from the South went for various reasons. Patrons stayed at these resorts ostensibly to cure themselves of certain diseases by drinking and bathing in the water there, to escape the sweltering heat and to mingle with wealthy men and women there.

It is easy to imagine that these resorts later became ideal places for eligible young men and women to meet and start a romance. The schedule of events included lessons in dancing, elaborate balls, cotillions and quiet walks around the grounds on summer nights. "Watering places" featured the finest in sumptuous atmospheres for noted Kentuckians like Henry Clay, Robert Breckinridge and John Hunt Morgan; prominent Kentuckians and other well-to-do southerners joined the upper crust of southern society here.

Later, Graham constructed a large hotel structure, "a splendid building costing upwards of $30,000 and capable of accommodating one thousand persons," one observer at the time noted. Graham Springs was well known throughout the South as the epitome of luxury.

One patron called Graham Springs "an elegant and commodious brick hotel." An important part of the atmosphere at Graham Springs was the music that wafted gently over the grounds. And George, Henry and Rueben, as talented musicians themselves, were a big part of those qualities that made Graham Springs special.

In the late fall and early winter, the three also became consummate waiters who plied their trade in the hotel restaurant and hotel itself. In a very real way, the three were very valuable in keeping the reputation of Graham Springs alive and before the wealthy.

Graham Sends Three to Do Concerts

Perhaps Graham wanted to send the three men on concert dates in New Albany and Madison, Indiana, and Cincinnati, Ohio, as harbingers of what was to come for the patrons of his establishment and broaden the appeal of his spa to southern Indiana. At any rate, he gave his trio a great deal of liberty, keeping the profits the men made, of course, while they played at various places around the area.

To Graham's surprise, the two slaves and free man of color taking the trip had other things on their minds than making music. In fact, when the three men boarded the steamboat *The Pike* to play dates on the Ohio River, they instead decided to escape to Canada.

The use of the steamboat as a means of escape for runaway slaves was a real problem in Kentucky, as more and more slaves were using the boats to run away from their masters. Something had to be done, slave owners said. So, in 1824 in Kentucky, the General Assembly enacted a law that said that the master of the steamboats was liable and could be criminally charged for transporting slaves "out of the limits of this state" without permission from the master. Later, the same body added liability for "the owner, mate, clerk, and engineer of any steam vessel."

The *Graham v. Strader* Case: The Slave as Property

A steamboat owned by Jacob Strader and James Gorman had transported George and two of Graham's slaves, Rueben and Henry, who then fled to freedom without Graham's permission.

According to Kentucky law, the steamboat company was liable for damages. Graham sued for $3,000 for the loss of the two slaves, plus $250 for musical instruments and $700 to $1,000 for books they left with; the total amount of the suit was to compensate Graham, who lost the slaves in a "fruitless efforts to recover them." Graham, of course, argued that he had lost a financial investment in the slaves, who were not only a source of labor but also a source of income.

Graham, it seems, had made a considerable effort to recover the two slaves. First, he sent his son, James, to look for the slaves in Cincinnati, but he couldn't find them. Next, he employed three men to follow the route the slaves took, starting in Louisville on *The Pike* and following the trail through Cincinnati and onto several small Ohio towns, eventually leading to Detroit, Michigan, and into Canada. Then Graham himself crossed over into Canada, but while there, he was set upon by a group of fugitive slaves who nearly killed him. Ultimately, he found his runaway slaves, but Graham could not convince them to return to Kentucky.

Accompanied by George, the free man of color, the runaway slaves resisted all Graham's entreaties to return to the Bluegrass State. So Graham then hired a free Louisville man of color named Shelton Morrisby, but he too could not convince the runaways to return. Apparently, George, Rueben and Henry lived out their lives as free men in Canada.

When all else failed, Graham sought restitution by filing a lawsuit. The opposition to the suit, Strader and Gorman, however, offered a unique defense. They argued that the two slaves were free anyway because they had spent a large block of time in free territory in what was known as the Northwest Ordinance, an area that was designated free territory by an enactment from the fledgling U.S. government itself. According to the defense, the time they had spent in the Northwest territory made Rueben and Henry free. So any lawsuit against the steamboat company was null and void, since no law forbad the free men from traveling on the steamboat.

Slaves, from Kentucky, for example, had been used in free territory to lay a crop by, but their masters were limited in the amount of time they were allowed to stay in free territory. But no slave had yet declared his freedom for living for a time in free territory.

Yet in deciding the case of *Strader v. Graham*, the ruling did not center on the slaves' freedom, as the Supreme Court regarded the slaves as property, not as human beings. After appeals to several lower courts, the case was brought before the highest court in Kentucky. The question the Supreme Court had to decide was whether Graham should be compensated for the financial loss he suffered due to his slaves escaping, using Strader and Gorman's steamboat as a means to run away. Ultimately, the court decided in Graham's favor, saying that he should be awarded $3,000 for his financial loss.

As to the matter of the slaves' freedom, the court declared that the slaves' time in a free state or territory did not qualify them for their freedom since they were slaves from Kentucky, and Kentucky's laws did indeed decide whether or not they were free. Under Kentucky law, they were not free. In other words, state law prevailed. The Graham case was less about slavery and more about financial compensation.

The Case as a Precedent for the Dred Scott Decision

Although the question of when a slave was free was ancillary to the overall case in the Graham suit, where financial compensation was the central question, the Dred Scott decision itself did hinge on a question in the Graham suit too: Was a slave free if he spent a time in a free state (Wisconsin in particular)? Justice Taney himself cited *Graham v. Strader* as a precedent in ruling that Dred Scott was not free: "[T]his court held that their [slaves'] status or condition, as free or slave, depended upon the laws, when they were brought back into that State, and that the court had no jurisdiction to revise the judgement of the court upon its own laws. This was the point directly before the court, and the decision that this court had no jurisdiction." Taney and the Supreme Court all turned on the will of the state. Turning to the Dred Scott case, Taney wrote, "As Scott was a slave when taken into the State of Illinois by his owner, and was there held as such, and brought back in that character, his status as free or slave, depended on the laws of Missouri [the master's residence], and not of Illinois." In this particular question, then, the Supreme Court used the case of *Strader v. Graham* in deciding the central question of the Dred Scott case: Was Dred Scott free since he had lived for a time in a free territory?

The court said no. Of course, that was not all the court said in its Dred Scott decision. Many were convinced that the decision went too far. So, what seemed a simple question in the *Strader v. Graham* turned out to be a decision that became the basis for one of the most important rulings in the country's history when, ultimately, Taney's extended remarks tore at the fabric of a nation and made the question of slavery an even knottier issue.

READING #4

THE OTHER THIRTEENTH AMENDMENT

AN ATTEMPT TO AVERT THE CIVIL WAR

Wasn't it the Thirteenth Amendment to the U.S. Constitution that freed the slaves? Not exactly. It depends on whether a person is referring to the earlier or later version of the Thirteenth Amendment. The early, unsuccessful Thirteenth Amendment did *not* free the slaves, but the latter, successful version did.

The story of what happened to each version of the Thirteenth Amendment is a story that most Americans don't know. The 2012 movie *Lincoln*, directed by Steven Spielberg, attempted to examine the careful politicking that Lincoln supervised to put this second Thirteenth Amendment on the road to ratification. In fact, he was successful, for this second version of the amendment was enacted in December 1865, after Lincoln's tragic death the preceding April.

What the movie doesn't detail is the Lincoln administration's desperate and unsuccessful attempt nearly four years earlier to restore the Union by amending the Constitution and preventing the Civil War through passage of this earlier version of the Thirteenth Amendment.

Yet understanding why the first attempt at enacting this earlier amendment failed needs explanation, including the role of several Kentuckians—even someone from Madison County—in the drama that led to the failure of the first Thirteenth Amendment.

Lincoln Dealt with a Split Party System. *Courtesy of Library of Congress.*

LINCOLN TAKES OFFICE

The Lincoln administration knew that when the "Great Emancipator" took office, it could not abolish slavery without amending the U.S. Constitution. In fact, Lincoln correctly felt that the country as a whole would find that any endeavor at manumitting slaves would result in a resounding defeat.

Truly, there was widespread opposition to emancipating the slaves in many states, including Kentucky. The people in what is now the Midwest feared that if the slaves were freed, former slaves would take jobs from White skilled workers. The upper New England area, too, was as generally resolute *for* freeing the slaves, led by Quakers, but pockets of opposition voiced the same fears against emancipating slaves as those in the Midwest. Little doubt exists that this kind of racial animosity would in the twenty-first century be called unadulterated racism.

To cite just one example, historian Leonard Richards, in *Who Freed the Slaves?*, details the beliefs of one of the strongest proponents for abolition, Senator James Ashley of Ohio, active for decades in illegally assisting slaves to escape bondage and a tireless leader in Congress for advocating the abolition of slavery.

But Senator Richards's attitudes toward Blacks seem today quite incongruous with his active efforts to free slaves. For instance, he believed that White people were more naturally intelligent than Black people, he was soundly against interracial marriage and he favored transporting all Black people out of the country "back to Africa." Yet he favored Blacks having the right to vote, to serve on juries and to join the military. To many in his day, Ashley was seen as radical in his convictions, but many today find more than a whiff of racism in his beliefs.

So as far as racial attitudes were concerned, at this point in the nineteenth century, racism reigned. All Lincoln and his fellow Republicans could do was limit slavery to those states that already had slavery and object to attempts to permit slavery in the territories that would become states, in the hopes that slavery would eventually die out.

Many people, like Kentucky senator Henry Clay and, to a degree, Lincoln himself, were members of a "colonialization" movement that advocated sending former slaves back to Africa as a way of dealing with African Americans and ridding the country of a maligned group.

As a result, Lincoln objected to the Crittenden Compromise. He saw the work of the Kentucky senator as a well-meaning attempt to prevent the dissolution of the Union that occurred after Lincoln was elected. That compromise, Lincoln reasoned, did not limit slavery to where it already existed and also provided for the possibility of slavery in the territories below a certain geographical line.

Lincoln hated slavery; he grew up thinking that way, and when he saw it firsthand, he concluded that if "slavery is not wrong, then nothing is wrong." But he knew that forbidding slavery in the territories was about all he could do, without some sort of amendment that would end slavery wherever it already existed.

In fact, Lincoln said, "I took [the oath of office] that I would, to the best of my abilities, preserve, protect, and defend the Constitution of the United States; it [was not my view] that I might take an oath [in fact] to get power and break the oath in using [that] power. [This oath] even forbade me to practically indulge my primary abstract judgment on the moral question of slavery," he wrote to A.G. Hodge of the *Frankfort Commonwealth* newspaper on April 4, 1864.

So, Lincoln reasoned then that his first job was to prevent the secession of states from what he saw as an indivisible Union. He saw that his primary purpose was to restore the Union first and then deal with slavery, if at all, later.

As Lincoln read the will of the majority of most Americans, in fact, no political will existed across most of the nation to emancipate the more than 3 million enslaved in the South. Those in the minority who desired to free the slaves had only the future to look to for any hopes of emancipation. If Lincoln and his fellow Republicans limited slavery to the Cotton South, the soil, in time, would no longer grow the cotton or any other crop that their economy was dependent on. Slavery, then, would eventually die.

Slavery in the Territories

Essentially, the nub of the issue that faced the country at the time of Lincoln's inauguration was not ending slavery, but rather, whether slavery would be allowed in the territories where the richer soils would grow better cotton and other cash crops. The South, we must imagine, saw limiting slavery to where it already existed as a serious blow to its economic health, a death knell to its unique way of life.

So this earlier Thirteenth Amendment did not mention that transplanting slavery to the territories was possible. In fact, it noted, "No amendment shall be made to the Constitution which will authorize or give Congress power to abolish or interfere within any State with the domestic institutions thereof, including that of persons held to labor or service by the laws of said State."

This Thirteenth Amendment, then, only covered slavery where it already existed. Naturally, because it did not allow for slavery in the territories, it became for the Deep South a bread-and-butter issue, a matter of the survival of the whole South as they saw it. To the South, expanding slavery to new ground was central to the South's unique way of life.

It had other effects too. Southerners of all stripes saw the unwillingness to allow for expansion in the territory issue as clear evidence that their fears were justified. To southerners, the North really wanted to end *all* slavery. Daniel W. Crofts's *Lincoln and the Politics of Slavery* records just a few of their reactions. For example, the citizens at the Lowndes County, Mississippi Courthouse "filled [it] to the brim" and "adopted resolutions that charged a number of our sister states with having violated both the spirit and letter of the Constitution by denying the South equal access to the territories with the slave system so as to promote servile insurrections…and by producing a spirit of hatred that could lead to civil war." Another source from Albany, Georgia, in a letter to his brother, expressed the fears of those other than the plantation owners: "The working class of men suspected that in the course of events the Negroes will be free and deprive them of their labor and become their equals." As Robert Holt, brother of Joseph Holt, an ardent Kentucky unionist, wrote to the newspaper the *Cloverport Democrat*, "White Southerners had heard endlessly that 'Black Republicans' planned to destroy slavery and confer equal citizen rights on ex-slaves." In Mississippi, the citizens were united, and he repeated the old belief that "[p]eople in the North were marked by dishonesty, injustice, rapacity, and an infernal greed." He continued, "[The secession movement] is a movement not of the leaders but of the masses whom the leaders could not control if they could. The conviction is strong and universal."

The Kentucky Legislature Debates the Old Thirteenth Amendment

Within Kentucky, a slave state, the opposition to the ratification voiced still other concerns. The most prominent spokesman was Lexingtonian John C. Breckinridge, now senator and former candidate on the Southern Democratic ticket for president. He reasoned that "Congress had no authority to ratify [the first Thirteenth Amendment] because seven states were unrepresented there." And besides, he reiterated, bowing to "reason," "the Republican Party had never claimed the power to interfere with slavery in the States."

Another legislator who also spoke against ratification of this earlier Thirteenth Amendment was Colonel George B. Hodge, who said that he "did not believe that the proposed amendment removed any cause of apprehension on the part of the people of Kentucky, for no such apprehension existed." He further objected to ratification because he did not believe that the amendment "evinced a disposition on the part of the North to do justice to the South."

But those who favored the ratification of the amendment had their say too. Madison County's Curtis F. Burnam "sharply rebutted" the claims of the Deep South. He noted that "Congress had acted legally, with far more than a quorum present." He then charged that "the Southern leadership had created a mass hysteria that wrongly convinced the Southern people that Republicans wanted to free all the slaves." Burnam concluded that he found it "amazing that gentlemen should now ignore the existence of a fact which… had been broadcast over the land." Burnam "condemned secessionists for refusing to recognize the amendment's assurance of permanent security to slavery in the States and pretended instead that no spirit of concession has ever been evinced by the North."

Because slavery in Kentucky was somewhat different than slavery in the Deep South, state legislatures there wanted to be sure that the Union would not interfere with their brand of slavery within the state. So, Kentucky became the first state to ratify the amendment. Unlike the Deep South, the state didn't need to expand slavery into the territories because the crops harvested by slaves in the state did not take the enormous acreage of extensive fields of cotton, sugar cane or rice, for example. In fact, Kentucky did a flourishing business selling its excess slaves to the Deep South, as mentioned earlier.

But in the end, the first Thirteenth Amendment in no way stemmed the tide of secession among Southern states or, for that matter, lured those seceded states back in the Union. In fact, after the war had begun, in rather meaningless gestures, only two other states, Ohio and Maryland, ratified the older form of the Thirteenth Amendment.

The Desperation of Offering the Older Thirteenth Amendment

Offering the amendment and Lincoln's support of it were desperate and rash moves. But Lincoln figured that he would at least give the amendment a chance in the hopes that it might be what the South wanted to hear and return to the Union.

Later in his administration, the second Thirteenth Amendment, as we now know it, became the focus of Lincoln's efforts. The administration rightly believed that some amendment to the Constitution was necessary to replace the Emancipation Proclamation, which Lincoln claimed was a military move and would not be in effect after the war.

Yet after four years of bloody war, with the country torn asunder, the Republicans did finally admit that slavery itself had been the underlying cause of the war. They must, in essence, eliminate it entirely, excise it from the body politic. With that in mind, they presented the second Thirteenth Amendment, which would free the slaves after being ratified by an appropriate number of states, with the majority being the seceded states.

Lincoln, in his second inaugural address, spoke eloquently about the past and the present: "All knew that this interest [slavery] was somehow the cause of the war. To strengthen, perpetuate, and extend this interest was the object for which the insurgents would rend the Union, even by war; while the government claimed no right to do more than restrict the territorial enlargement of it." But Lincoln's acknowledgement of the earlier beliefs of the seceded states was not replete with harsh words and hateful recrimination; he called for "malice toward none; with charity for all; with firmness in the right, as God gives us to see the right, let us strive on to finish the work we are in; to bind up the nation's wounds…to do all which may achieve and cherish a just, and a lasting peace, among ourselves, and with all nations."

While he did not specifically name the aborted Thirteenth Amendment, he did reassure all that his mercy, not his anger, would guide the future. But in less than a month, he would be dead, and the retaliation of Reconstruction became the hated scourge of both the North and the South. Contrary to Lincoln's wishes, there was much malice and little mercy to all.

READING #5

KENTUCKIANS, THE 1850 FUGITIVE SLAVE LAW AND CASS COUNTY, MICHIGAN

All wars have several causes, and historians seem to agree that the Civil War had many. Historians cite, among others, the growing distrust in the South of the power of the North to control the political life of people in the South. It was a question of states' rights, the argument goes. They also name the increasing popularity of the abolitionist movement seeking to abolish slavery. The increase in taxes on cotton shipped from the South also frustrated the large plantation owners in the cotton-growing regions.

Then there was the publication in 1852 of Harriet Beecher Stowe's *Uncle Tom's Cabin*; John Brown's attack on the arsenal at Harper's Ferry, Virginia, in 1859; and the publicity surrounding Kentucky slave Margaret Garner's 1856 killing of her own child rather than living life as a slave—all focused on the inherent evils of slavery.

In his second inaugural address, in March 1865, President Abraham Lincoln saw slavery as the principal cause of the conflict, for slavery, in essence, was at the center of nearly every issue the South debated with the North. Lincoln was clear: "All knew that this interest [slavery] was somehow the cause of the war." The South feared that the political power of the North would eventually lead to the freeing of the slaves. The increase in taxes on cotton also meant that slavery would not be as profitable for plantation owners. The abolitionist movement, of course, also struck at the heart of the issue of slavery.

PRACTICAL ILLUSTRATION OF THE FUGITIVE SLAVE LAW.

Many Objected to the Fugitive Slave Law. *Courtesy of Library of Congress.*

Alexander Stephens, vice president of the Confederate States of America, admitted that the South was a "slavocracy," dependent on slavery for its very foundation.

THE VALUE OF A SLAVE TO A SLAVE OWNER

It's not surprising that, to slave owners, slaves were quite valuable. To lose a slave was to lose a valuable source of income, as despicable as we find slavery today. According to economists Samuel Williamson and Louis Cain, a ready-to-work enslaved field hand averaged about $20,000 in today's dollars, plus there was the expense of maintaining him or her. Older slaves and children, of course, were valued at less, but all had to be fed, housed, clothed and cared for when ill or injured. Slaves with advanced skills like carpenters, coopers, barbers and blacksmiths, for instance, cost more, and female slaves generally were a bit more expensive because they could have children and produce even more slaves.

According to historical statistics, male slaves lived to an average of 35.54 years, females slightly longer at 38.08 years—both dying much younger than Whites of the same period. To make matters even worse, slaves had no real rights. They could not vote, legally marry, testify in court or exercise any rights as a citizen that Whites had. The slave masters controlled the very existence of the slave, who was regarded as chattel, to be bought and sold and treated at the whim and caprice of the slave owner.

By 1840, the United States had 2,483,721 slaves. In the same year, Kentucky had 182,258 slaves, representing 23.37 percent of a population of 779,828. So, about one in four persons in Kentucky in 1840 was a slave.

Obviously, slaves across the South sought escape, either by means of the Underground Railroad or by themselves in attempts to flee from such despicable conditions. Historian Lisa Vox estimates that by 1850, 100,000 slaves from across the South had escaped bondage. Other estimates are lower than that, but there was no doubt to slave owners that runaway slaves were a problem. Kentucky, of course, sat geographically on the border between the North and South, with many escaping slaves crossing its borders.

Under the sway of a powerful southern lobby, and because slavery existed even in the North at the time, the early founders of the republic recognized the cost of losing a slave. Consequently, a law enacted in 1793, the Fugitive Slave Act, required ordinary citizens to assist in the return of runaway slaves. Yet the early law soon lost much of its force as more and more northern states outlawed slavery. In fact, the statute was largely ineffective as more northern juries and law enforcement officials refused to enforce it, using local statutes as grounds for ignoring the law.

By the antebellum period, slave owners in the South wanted action to stop the flow of escaped slaves and their return to their slave masters. To them, something must be done.

Most Kentuckians don't know that two incidents involving Kentuckians from Bourbon and Boone Counties were significant in leading to the enactment of one of the most onerous laws ever passed by Congress: the 1850 Fugitive Slave Law. This law severely penalized local officials, in the North and South, for not capturing an alleged runaway slave and returning him to his or her master. This was based on the testimony of the owner only—the slave had no right to dispute the testimony of a White person. Those who assisted in the capture were rewarded financially for their work. Those who impeded capture paid a very stiff penalty. Northerners cynically called it the "Bloodhound Law," and many states refused to enforce the statute.

Incidents in Cass County Michigan

Kentucky had long been concerned with the fugitive slave problem within the state. Marion Lucas's book on the history of Black people in Kentucky notes that after 1830, "increasing agitation of the slavery question at the national level led to new enactments. Over the next 30 years the legislature increased the fees paid for apprehending fugitives and provided stiffer penalties for those convicted for enticing slaves to escape." How much of a problem was runaway slaves in the Commonwealth? In *Speculators and Slaves*, Michael Tadman estimates that in the 1850s in Kentucky, between 46 and 79 enslaved people escaped to freedom yearly. When figured in dollars and cents, those figures were quite high, running a minimum from $92,000 to $158,000 in today's dollars.

Tensions, then, ran high in the state over the runaway slave problem. H.E. Everman's two-part history of Bourbon County observed that the county earlier flirted with emancipation moves and supported the "colonialization" movement of the U.S. senator and national leader, Henry Clay, an extremely popular Kentucky politician. But in the 1840s, the county was seeing "changing slavery attitudes," with politicians openly defending "the slavery institution." In fact, the Bourbon County court gave "increasing attention to [slave] patrols, not only in Paris, but also in Millersburg and even Flat Rock." Garrett Davis, a leading politician in the county and later important at the state and national levels, stressed his support of "property rights as guaranteed by the Constitution." Davis even, as Everman noted, "wrote a strong amendment assuring the high legal status of slave property." The attitude in Bourbon County, as it was in most of the rest of the South, was that slaves were mere "property" and that slave owners had a right to protect their "property rights" by retaining and thus *retrieving* their "property" whenever slave owners' rights had been violated.

It was a frame of mind that no doubt provided some of the impetus for a group of Bourbon County slave owners who had lost slaves and were anxious to retrieve their "property." According to Benjamin Wilson, writing in *Michigan History*, the stories of thriving fugitive slave communities in Cass County, Michigan, and nearby communities probed the very essence of the slavery problem at the national level. His extensive research documents the cultural, legal and ethical divides between these two sections of the country that indirectly led to the passage of the 1850 Fugitive Slave Act.

Wilson speculates that southerners, in this case Kentuckians in particular, learned that a number of runaway slaves lived in the Cass

County, Michigan area and were successful in their endeavors as farmers and productive members of that society. An article appeared in the *Ledger*, a New Albany, Indiana proslavery newspaper, published just across the river from Louisville, Kentucky, a slave state, that typifies the kind of piece that would have infuriated slave owners who had lost slaves. The article said, in part, "There is in Cass County, Michigan, a large settlement of colored people, mostly from the Southern states. They have a fine location, well-tilled farms, neat and comfortable cottages and buildings, and live an industrious and happy life."

Wilson noted that in the winter of 1847, some "planters" from Bourbon County, Kentucky, decided they would do something about their runaway problem, speculating that their runaway slaves had fled to Cass County. But to be sure, they verified their suspicions by sending a young man they called "Carpenter" to Cass County to try to affirm their speculations that some of their runaway slaves were living and even prospering in Cass County.

"Carpenter" first posed as an abolitionist from Massachusetts in order to secure the confidence of the local people, Quakers, in particular, who were involved in placing runaway slaves in the southern Michigan area. Gleaning useful information, "Carpenter" then disguised himself as a canvasser for an abolitionist newspaper in order to verify just who the runaways were and where they were located, information he quickly passed on to his coconspirators back home in Bourbon County, Kentucky.

Late in August 1847, thirteen residents of Bourbon County formed a raiding party intent on retrieving their runaway slaves, sure now where they lived and who was protecting them. At first, they tried to establish their headquarters at Battle Creek, Michigan, but soon met with hostility toward slave catchers and were forced to move their headquarters to Bristol, Indiana, just about an hour south of Cass County.

On August 16, traveling at night and heavily armed, the raiders divided into three groups: one group to hold hostage the family the Kentuckians saw as the leaders of a "headquarters" for the abolitionist movement in the area, to keep them from alerting the local citizenry. Two other groups formed raiding parties. One of the two raiding parties soon "seized their prey," except for some who fled and headed back to their headquarters. The second raiding party, set to retrieve their runaway slaves, was led by Reverend A. Stevens, who claimed that some of his runaways had settled in Cass County. That group ran into some problems.

Stevens found that his runaways were indeed living in Cass County, but when he knocked, the residents recognized his voice and refused to open the door. Angered by their resistance, Stevens wielded an axe, tore down the door, wounded the husband and succeeded in capturing his "property." Confident, he then headed to the rendezvous point to meet the other two parties and then head back to Kentucky.

Unfortunately for Stevens, the local citizenry had gotten word of the raiding and were able to capture him. Taunted vigorously for abducting a mother and her child and being a clergyman, he was forced to parade before the citizenry to the point that the preacher "actually cried with vexation." Taken before the local circuit court judge, the Kentuckians were indicted for "attempted kidnapping and assault and battery," and the runaway slaves were set free.

The Kentuckians, feeling aggrieved at what they saw as a miscarriage of justice, employed an attorney to adjudicate the case in the local court. The court, however, was not sympathetic, freeing the fugitives again, who then promptly fled to Canada to avoid any more trouble.

But the Bourbon Countians didn't give up their legal fight and filed another suit against a number of Cass Countians in U.S. District Supreme Court to "recover the value of their property." Wilson related, however, that the Kentuckians won their suit, "but their attorneys took all the money as fees." Although the Cass County defendants certainly won a moral victory, they were left with financial costs to pay that, in spite of community support, resulted in crippling debt for many. But the incident sparked interest in the plight of runaways in the area and resulted in local laws designed to protect the rights of Black residents.

But as expected, the plight of the Bourbon County slave owners and their subsequent lawsuits ignited a firestorm of backlash not only in Kentucky but also throughout the South, with slave owners demanding protection of their "property rights." In this atmosphere, slave owner John Norris of Boone County, Kentucky, learned that some of his runaways, David Powell and family, were living in Cass County too. Norris quickly decided to retrieve his fugitives.

With eight fellow raiders, Norris arrived in Cass County on September 27, 1849, and located David Powell's home. The raiders forcibly entered the home and captured a number of members of the Powell family, one of whom objected that he was married to a free woman. They promised the slave that his wife could also return to Kentucky with her husband, "guaranteeing the spouse would be well treated in the South." Quickly, all the captives were bound, and the party set out for Kentucky. But they were intercepted by an angry party in South Bend, Indiana, hauled into court and charged with "riotous activities and other breaches of civil processes." While in the courtroom, Norris quickly concluded that the large group of supporters for the fugitives would soon take control of the situation. So, he "gathered his men around the captives, seized them with one hand, brandished their weapons with the other and threatened to shoot anyone who would attempt to take away their property." But realizing the impossibility of their stand, the Kentuckians relented and released their captives. They then put away their weapons, but the judge quickly freed the captured fugitives and returned them to Cass County, where they, too, were were soon off to Canada.

Also seeking justice in the judicial system, Norris filed suit in U.S. Circuit Court on December 21, 1849. The court awarded him more than $10,000 from the Indiana abolitionists who had prevented him from retrieving his runaway slaves.

But the implications of the two raids were clear: the South demanded more protection against shielding runaways, and the North soon enacted a whole series of complex "personal liberty" laws that greatly countered the intent of the statutes that protected the "property" of slave owners. Wilson noted, for example, that Senator Henry Clay "cited the 1847 Michigan Riot in Cass County as an example of the need to provide adequate protection for southern slaveholders." Events like those involving Kentuckians intent on recovering their runaway slaves led to the Fugitive Slave Act of 1850, a piece of legislature that hardened attitudes toward slavery both North and South, mindsets that led to the Civil War just eleven years later.

Few Kentuckians today realize the role that those raids in Bourbon and Boone Counties had on the terrible conflict that engulfed the nation and redefined the essential nature of the United States.

READING #6

BENNETT YOUNG

THE ST. ALBANS RAID AND THE "LOST CAUSE"

Bennett Young is quite important in Kentucky Civil War history for many different reasons. He is, of course, best recognized as the organizer and leader of the famous St. Albans, Vermont raid, the deepest penetration of the Confederacy during the course of the war. All told, on October 19, 1864, he and his men were responsible for robbing the three banks in town that netted $208,000, a bold move and only fifteen miles from the U.S.-Canada border.

The Confederates sought to divert attention away from the activities of Generals William Tecumseh Sherman and "Little Phil" Sheridan and, at the same time, raise necessary funds for the Confederacy. It hardly worked. The daring raid quickly became an international incident that tied up legal experts on either side of the border, trying to sort out whether the incident was an "act of war" or just a group of twenty-one Confederates seeking to fill their own coffers with much-needed cash.

But to dismiss Bennett Young as just the author of the raid of an erstwhile band of alien Rebels—and get away with it—grossly underestimates the importance of Young to the Confederacy during the war and long after it. The measure of the man is much more complex.

Bennett Young's Early Days in the War

Born on May 25, 1843, into a family of heroes of the Revolutionary War in rural Jessamine County, Kentucky, near Nicholasville, Bennett Young

Bennett Young Advocates for Slavery. *Courtesy of Library of Congress.*

was a mere eighteen-year-old when he, along with many friends and neighbors, joined Company B of Colonel Roy Cluke of the 8th Kentucky Cavalry, CSA.

Soon Cluke's troops had earned themselves a sizable reputation for efficiency and victory. Historian Sam Flora noted that that Cluke and his men "destroy[ed] over one million dollars of Federal supplies" and "disrupted communication," while gaining valuable experience as well as the attention of Confederate General John Hunt Morgan, who quickly invited Cluke and his men to be a part of what was later called "Morgan's Great Raid" into parts of Indiana and Ohio, beginning in Burkesville, Kentucky, on July 2, 1863. Morgan and his men, including Young, crossed into "Yankee Land" at Brandenburg and immediately met opposition at Corydon, Indiana, a pattern that repeated itself all the way to West Point, Ohio. Morgan and what was left of his men surrendered on July 26, 1863, after a grueling and exhausting series of skirmishes, firefights and a long journey as far as eastern Ohio.

Lester Horwitz's *The Longest Raid* explains that Young, along with some fellow prisoners, were first assigned to prison at Camp Chase and later transferred to Camp Douglas near Chicago. The conditions at the latter prison were deplorable, with mistreatment of inmates common, delivered with harsh and unforgiving discipline. Young tried to escape once, spent time in the dungeon and, eventually, as Flora noted, bribed a guard into effecting a successful escape.

After spending time on a ship running a Yankee blockade, Young eventually enrolled at the University of Toronto. Young impressed fellow Confederates enough to convince the Confederate government in Richmond, Virginia, of his usefulness as a "special operations" officer who could plan and guide operations in various nefarious activities in the United States for the Confederate cause. That cause included the St. Albans Raid.

More Information on the St. Albans Raid

The raid at St. Albans was typical for its extensive preparation, something that impressed superiors. All alone, Bennett Young drifted into St. Albans toting a Bible. He was assumed to be a "man of the cloth." Leisurely, his other men, never stirring any curiosity, made their way into this sleepy northern Vermont village.

On the day of the robberies, some of Young's men kept the most prominent citizens at gunpoint while the remainder robbed the three banks in town. Bennett Young himself announced, "I am an officer of the Confederate service who is going to take this town." The whole operation, according to Michelle Arnosky Sherburne's *The St. Albans Raid*, had a rather lighthearted lilt to it and produced three vignettes not often cited when the action is discussed.

In one instance, an eighty-year-old man, oblivious to what was happening, thought that the robbers were quite "rude," never once realizing that the bank was being robbed. Second, another robber made the people in one of the banks swear allegiance to the Confederacy in his zeal to impress the patrons with his power. Third, the Confederates were going to set the town on fire using "Greek fire" but were only successful in setting an outhouse on fire. No word on whether or not someone was in it.

Later, Young could not resist taunting the little town, requesting copies of the local newspaper's account of the raid but enclosing money to pay for his hotel bill while in St. Albans. In fact, Young identified the whole raid as the "5th Company Confederate Retributors" to emphasize that part of his mission of the robberies was in part a way to exact revenge for the harsh treatment he and his fellow prisoners received while in military prisons.

Sometimes he referred to his actions at St. Albans as the "Vermont Yankee Scare Party," another indication of his purpose to bring the war to even the "least suspicious." While the operation in St. Albans was well planned, the robbers thought that a swift ride over the Canadian border would lose their pursuers; instead, a posse from St. Albans caught up with one group of robbers and were about to hang them when Canadian authorities stepped in to take the robbers to jail.

According to *Confederate Operations in Canada and New York*, after protracted international negotiations, years later, even Bennett Young was free from blame, and the Canadian government had "no case" even against Young; it dropped all charges, noting that "this noted prisoner departed in peace." In fact, while much of the money from the robbery was returned, the Confederates still kept a substantial portion of it. By that time, strong public opinion in Canada had swung in the Confederates' favor, and his soldiers themselves became in the eyes of most Canadians nice, well-raised and well-mannered boys from prominent Kentucky families.

His Time Spent After the War

At the close of the war, for three years, Young was not welcomed back in the States. He used these three years wisely, studying law for two years at the University of Edinburgh and at Queen's University of Ireland until President Andrew Johnson granted ex-Confederates amnesty. Then Young returned to Louisville, where he quickly built up a thriving law practice, "one of the largest law practices in the South," biographer Flora noted.

Young, however, did not confine himself just to the practice of law. He devoted himself to a number of civic causes, including helping to found or fund the Louisville Free Public Library, the Filson Club, the Kentucky School for the Blind and the Orphan School for Girls. He used his skill in law to assist the Colored Orphan Home and the Booker T. Washington Community Center, as well as promoting better race relations for African Americans in the city.

Young's Work on the "Lost Cause" Movement

Nonetheless, he is probably most well-known as one of the chief spokespersons for the "Lost Cause," a movement in the defeated South to record in history that the Confederacy had fought the valiant fight for a noble cause against overwhelming odds for a way of life that the North was intent on destroying. To the believers, the cause of the war was hardly slavery, as the slaves flourished in a paternal system that granted slaves the advantages of modern civilization, including primitive Christianity. In this belief system, without the venal actions of most Union generals, in a *fair* fight, the South's highly developed system of agriculture would have easily triumphed.

Following the war was Reconstruction, when Carpetbaggers from the North did all they could to destroy the southern way of life and impose the "immorality" of the northern economic system.

The venerated Southern generals like Robert E. Lee and Kentuckian Albert Sidney Johnston became symbols of the cavalier spirit in military and civilian life. Various societies like the Daughters of the Confederacy, Sons of the Confederacy and the United Confederate Veterans Association and publications like *Confederate Veteran*, published in Louisville, spread this reading of staunch supporters of the movement.

Kentucky, which according to popular parlance "joined" the Confederacy after the war, elected a long series of Confederate military men to the governorship and was at the forefront of the "Lost Cause" movement at the time. And Bennett Young was one of its most ardent and popular spokesmen—known, in fact, as one "of the greatest orators of the Lost Cause." One listener in an article from the *Louisville Journal* concluded that "no other speaker could move the Confederate heart like this Kentuckian." He is said to be responsible for the General Zollicoffer Monument at Mill Springs Battlefield, saving the Jefferson Davis home in Todd County, the erection of the Jefferson Davis Monument in Fairview and the establishment of the Kentucky Confederate Veteran Home in Peewee Valley, Kentucky.

While Young is most famous for his support of Confederate causes, the St. Albans Raid, as well as his book *Wizards of the Saddle* and his many community, state and region activities mark him as one of Kentucky's most civic-minded citizens. In truth, though, Young believed that the "Lost Cause" movement should include slavery. In fact, slavery in any form was an integral part of the plan.

READING #7

THE BEREA INCIDENT

THE FEAR OF SLAVE OWNERS IN MADISON COUNTY

According to many Civil War historians, the one common fear many slave owners felt was the fear of slave insurrections. In many ways, their fear was realistic. Over the years, several unsuccessful slave rebellions have been a part of American history.

According to Harvard's Henry Louis Gates, possibly the premier Black historian, thirty-three rebellions of ten or more slaves are recorded in American history, beginning with the Stono Rebellion in 1739 and continuing all throughout the early and middle part of the nineteenth century.

JOHN BROWN'S RAID

The most famous of these rebellions was the Nat Turner Rebellion in Virginia, which climaxed with a highly significant but unsuccessful insurrection at Harper's Ferry, Virginia, commonly called "John Brown's Raid" on October 16–18, 1859.

Brown's purpose was to incite rebellion among the local slaves that would ultimately spread to all the enslaved South, destroying slavery wherever it existed in one God-inspired insurrection. Of course, Brown was unsuccessful and was captured and hanged. (Incidentally, Brown was captured by Robert E. Lee.) Brown and his devotees felt that after the slaughter at Lawrence, Kansas, by those advocating slavery, nonviolence and talk yielded little.

Much Turmoil Characterized the Civil War. *Courtesy of Library of Congress.*

Unlike others, Brown's Raid was reported nationally, alerting the entire nation of the events at Harper's Ferry to a country already caught in the inevitable throes of forceful debate over the slavery question.

THE CRISIS REACHES A BOILING POINT

After many contentious years, it was a debate whose time had come. For different reasons, Brown's trial and subsequent hanging were significant news in both the North and South. Already, Illinois senator Stephen Douglas had advocated "popular sovereignty" in what was called "Bleeding Kansas," where the residents of the state were to determine whether or not they would permit slavery. The result was a bloodbath all across the territory, not just in Lawrence.

John Brown and his followers felt that the time for revenge was upon them—this time, they felt, with God on their side. As Brown said ominously at his trial, "I, John Brown, am now certain that the crimes of this guilty land will never be purged away, but with Blood." Slave owners across the South suddenly placed restrictions on slaves by not allowing them any privileges that they normally had. Some, for example, prohibited slaves from assembling in churches. Some suspected any slave who met with groups of other slaves. According to Marion Lucas's study, "Rumors spread that authorities were going to round up all the black preachers and sell them 'down the river,'" a fate all slaves were horrified by.

The Effect on Madison County

In Madison County, Kentucky, for instance, unlike before, slaves were not permitted out after dark, even if carrying notes from their masters allowing them to move about freely. In addition, groups of White men patrolled the area, desperately ferreting out even the slightest trouble from the slaves. In fact, the county, like the country, was awash with rumors of an impending revolution.

It was no exaggeration to say that Brown's raid caused the nation to keenly focus on the question of slavery. Few events had the impact of this raid. Already, Madison County had clear dividing lines. In 1860, 35.9 percent of the people were slaves, tending hemp, tobacco and various other crops mostly in the northern part of the county. In the southern part of the county, John Fee, on land given to him by county resident and "firebrand emancipationist" Cassius Clay, began a coeducational and integrated school.

Fee described the school's mission by saying that "the best way to inspire [a] woman, colored or white, with virtuous sentiments, and establish in her habits of purity, was not to treat her invidiously—shut her up in pens, schools by herself, but treat her like all women of respectability and thus inspire her with hope and noble resolve, and lift her above the seductive influences of a vicious life." Such revolutionary thinking was much to the chagrin of neighboring farmers, who delivered their opinions with threats and other forms of intimidation, including mob violence.

The Fears of Southern Madison County

The events at Harper's Ferry only added to Madison Countians' fears that Fee and his work, his preaching in various places in and around the area against slavery, his devoted followers and his revolutionary ideas would bring the wrath down on residents in the southern Madison County area by slave owners. While slavery was not as prevalent in the southern part of the county, the residents there not among John Fee's followers reasoned that they were not safe in their homes as long as these so-called abolitionists were present and part of the community.

Adding to their disdain and concern was a "summary" in George Prentice's *Louisville Journal* of a sermon Fee delivered at Henry Ward Beecher's church, asking for more funds from his Boston congregants to support Fee's efforts. Prentice quipped sarcastically, "John Fee [was] in Beecher's church calling for more John Brown's." Fee maintained that he had been misquoted.

Soon a number of concerned citizens called a meeting in Richmond at the courthouse where sixty planters decided that these abolitionists, including Fee, had to leave the county. Many of those same people who were asked to leave had earlier moved to Berea to be missionaries. In particular, many were there to work with the non-slaveholding Whites who were often illiterate and poor themselves, living in substandard houses, who had moved to Berea to take advantage of the schools and the churches.

At first Fee and his devotees appealed to Governor Beriah Magoffin, himself a Southern sympathizer, for protection. But the governor had little sympathy with their cause and told them that the state government would not shield them; he advised them that the best that they could do was to leave the state. The governor, it seemed, was more concerned about the events at Harper's Ferry and their effect on the Commonwealth and could not "engage to protect these Berea residents from their fellow citizens." So, in late December 1859, thirty-six exiles, stripped of their property and means of livelihood, arrived in Cincinnati, having been expelled from their Berea homes. The *Cincinnati Inquirer* described their arrival in the Queen City as finding the "pilgrims" in "fine-spirits."

Fee's Action during the War

Fee tried several times to return to Berea, but each time he was met with angry mobs. Some exiles, however, after the war, returned to Berea. Meanwhile, during the war, Fee turned his attention to Camp Nelson, where he assisted in training and caring for Black soldiers and their families. At the same time, Berea College survived, and Fee's dream of a church and a school for poor White and Black students became a reality.

Would all of the events that confronted the people of Madison County have happened if John Brown had not raided Harper's Ferry? It is difficult to say, but the Civil War itself was as sure as any event in U.S. history.

READING #8

WAR WEARINESS AND THE ENIGMA OF WAR

The craggy, old-looking face, the thinning hair and the deep-set eyes cry out that age and worry are frequent visitors here. His hair is in place, but it lacks the bouncy vibrancy of a young man trying to keep it orderly. The face is familiar enough, but the visage has truly changed. Where once the fifty-six-year-old man's image radiated hope and optimism for a nation at war with itself, now all the concerns of the same nation seem embedded in the deep grooves in his face, running diagonally from his forehead to the chin.

This is, of course, one of the last photographs of Abraham Lincoln—an image that begs for sympathy. In fact, it virtually cries out for some recognition of what all he has met.

Knowing his concerns of the last four years, reflective surprise seems inappropriate. Surely, part of his face shows the tragic death of his son, yet somehow the greater part mirrors the long and sleepless nights, the disappointments of trips to the telegraph office and the tedious yet entirely necessary conversations with generals too often concerned with their own egos and less with their country and men's interests. Surely, the cares of the world seem to rest on his face.

For Lincoln was, above all else, war weary, ground down gradually by all the fire and fury, the unseemly and useless death and destruction. The photographs of war that appeared in the press captured, for many for the first time, all the horrors of battle. Bloody battles haunt his tortured soul. But the president was indeed not the only person affected by the cruel ravages of war.

Liberty Was Tested. *Courtesy of Library of Congress.*

Many others, both in the South and North, showed similar deep disappointments and weariness. Historian Drew Faust's recent work on death and the American psyche, *The Republic of Suffering*, graphically records that weariness in both soldiers and citizens. In fact, just looking at just Kentucky warriors, Confederate and Union, the war affected a number of soldiers in many ways. "War is hell," General William Tecumseh said—a sentiment shared not just by Kentuckians but by many others.

It Began Quite Early and Lasted Long According to Those in Power

General Robert Anderson, the "Hero of Fort Sumter," saw that the world was too much with the Louisvillian. Anderson's hollow and deep-set eyes knew that the "irresistible conflict," as Secretary William Seward had predicted, had arrived, and Anderson himself felt, perhaps wrongly, responsible for it. In his early days, as he confessed to his wife in a letter, war was confusing to him: "I think no more absurd scheme could be invented for settling national difficulties than the one we are engaged in—killing each other to find out who is in the right." In fact, appointed on May 15, 1861, to command the

Department of Kentucky, he resigned a short time later on October 8, 1861, lasting only briefly amid his lingering doubts and indecisiveness.

War wore on others too. Confederate General Basil Duke looked on the face of his brother-in-law and commander General John Hunt Morgan and remarked that Morgan "had greatly changed. His face wore a weary, care-worn expression and his manner was destitute of its former ardor and enthusiasm." For General John Hunt Morgan, for years a dashing Southern cavalier raider, the "Thunderbolt of the Confederacy," all commitment to a just cause had seemed to have passed; in truth, he approached his swashbuckling raids with a dulled and contagious pessimism.

Early and Late Attempts to Blame

Louisville Union General John Pope's commander complained bitterly about Pope's men who under his leadership "believe they have a perfect right to rob, tyrannize, threaten and maltreat anyone they please." To that observer, his candid assessment was that the war had brutalized the soldiers themselves rather than made them the gracious victors intricately involved in a moral cause. Instead, Pope's soldiers, his commander said, "had lost their bearings on the firing line and entered into a brutal struggle, predicated upon something close to criminal intent." To the public, war, too, had dulled the dignity and deep regard for the soldier.

Especially in the border states of Missouri and Kentucky, some former Southern soldiers turned into bloodthirsty guerrillas accustomed to appropriating what they needed, as Klotter observed. Some treated this as a temporary expedient, but others had acquired a taste for violent adventure that "became incurable." Such guerrilla activity was largely carried out by disaffected soldiers too eager to use "military might" to get anything they wanted in spite of its having (or not having) usefulness or "military purposes." To this group, it was killing, robbing and mayhem for the pure sport of it. Bedlam for bedlam's sake, they espoused.

But according to State Historian Dr. Klotter, guerrilla activity was "the everyday experience" of most law-abiding citizens in the Commonwealth, always aware that such guerrilla activity was imminent. Today could be the day, the ordinary citizen thought.

Many guerrillas, frustrated by the dictatorial rule of Union General Stephen Burbridge, reasoned that their presence was less harmful to the Commonwealth than what Burbridge had done. To them, they had no other choice but to strike back in reckless abandon. But Burbridge's draconian tactics were too much for everyday Kentuckians. Often the Kentucky citizenry, the guerrillas and Burbridge's war on them were nothing more than bloodthirsty acts of revenge for both sides—with neither side winning.

Unfortunately, even the normal activities of war seemed to have a questionable purpose. Captain Nathaniel Southgate Shaler of the 5th Kentucky Artillery (U.S.) described a moment when fellow officers watched a Union sharpshooter kill a Confederate sitting on a roof sketching the Union position: "The [Union] sniper drills the boy through the head. As the face slips out of sight, we see the startled look that comes upon a man [the Confederate] who suddenly knows [his own] death." To Shaler, though, the killing seemed more like murder than military conflict. He was suddenly repulsed by what his own marksman had done in war's name. The marksman walked away, in Shaler's words, "taking care he does not look into the officers' eyes." In fact, Shaler concluded that "[war] seems neither holy nor noble, but hard, brutal fight [t]hat bears the soul right down. War is hell's part, not heaven's; Sherman was right."

Later, in the white heat of battle itself, the same Shaler recalled the brutality of combat: "The heat from roasting gun barrels had created a convection current above the battery, swirling body parts, eyeballs, teeth, shards of uniform and equipment through the air, and they were blown out, rent by [a] hurricane [of] bits and shreds that spatter down to earth what once were good men—friends and foes alike." In a similar vein, Stuart Sanders of the Kentucky Historical Society cited a letter from a Union soldier, John T. Harrington of the Kentucky (U.S.) 22nd Infantry Regiment, who seems to say what many Kentucky soldiers felt: "I have seen war in all of its horrors." Harrington was even more particular: "I have been in the fierce charge amidst the shouts of victory and felt myself on the pinnacle of glory. I have lain perfectly exhausted among the wounded and the dead. I have seen agony in its slightest as well as its most acute form, and I have been among the number fleeing before a victorious enemy and all through the cursed blunders of a set of political demigods [political generals] with straps on their shoulders."

DEATH WAS NOT THE ONLY ALTERNATIVE

The half-dead, the maimed and the permanently injured continued to live the war's brutality long after the guns were silent. In truth, the magnitude of the destruction of the human body can only be reduced to numbers to imagine its deleterious effects.

Douglas Adams's *Living Hell* cites some of these very telling numbers: "In 1867 alone federal medical authorities purchased 4,095 prosthetic legs, 2391 arms, 61 hands, and 14 feet. In the first postwar year, Mississippi spent half of its state's budget on artificial limbs." Yet even with these figures, it is impossible to calculate the human misery and loss of productivity surviving veterans suffered—the ex-soldier with the flat sleeve or wooden leg, the lifetime of disability.

Death Lingered Like an Uninvited Specter

Death was all around. In war, there is no way to avoid it. After battle, bodies of friend and foe lie scattered on the field, often so thick that soldiers found it frustrating—stepping around them, carefully avoiding them, if possible—with their open eyes staring blankly at a cloudy sky.

And it wasn't just this war. It was other wars too. The same General Robert Anderson, explaining his deep questions about military conflict, spoke of his experiences in the Black Hawk War: "The misery exceed[ed] any I ever expected to see in our happy land. Dead bodies, males and females, strewn along the road, left unburied, expected." And where there is death there is the acrid smell of busy maggots working on consuming a lifeless body in blue or gray. Kentuckian General Kenner D. Garrard even told of retrieving a blanket and finding a "horde of friendly hatched maggots that groped blindly over his body," eager to begin the process of consuming his body.

To Many, War Is Sometimes Completely Justified

Sometimes, as revolting it may seem, war seems to be the only choice. This is not to say that all these fighting men were to many people not without considerable honor, for all during the years prior to the actual Civil War they had spent decades wrangling with their opposition. To many, then, the Civil War was inevitable; Kentuckian Henry Clay and others might have delayed it in 1820 and 1850, but the march of the entire country was toward some sort of armed conflict, some way of settling issues on the field of battle over what had become unsolvable in the courts of law or the halls of Congress. War, they reasoned, was unavoidable.

Many of the older generation applauded what the living and dying soldiers had done. One ex-Connecticut soldier lauded the soldier for his long-suffering patience, as noted by Lonn in *Desertion in the Civil War*: "He is a better and stronger man for having fought three years out-facing death and suffering. Like the nation, he has developed and learned his powers." In truth, many soldiers, blue and gray, lived long and productive lives, molding the rest of their days after battle in great patriotic consonance with the nation's optimistic direction after the war.

War, they reasoned, was necessary, despite all its horrors. They were not advocates of war, but sometimes war is the only way.

The Curious Enigma of War

To some, war wears on a person no matter the depth of his commitment, prompting some men to question in deepest moments of reflection, concluding that there must be another way.

The South Was Idyllic. *Courtesy of Library of Congress.*

The "grand havoc of battle" will probably always be alluring and intoxicating to the young. The glorious win over the opposition, watching him skedaddle over the bloodstained plain; the inevitable camaraderie of like-minded men who become brothers in arms; and the deep satisfaction of accomplishing a noble victory do, indeed, attract young men like bees to honey. Glory can be theirs, they think. Then their names and bravery will go down in the halls of heroes, they reason. "I shall be known and revered," they say.

But Confederate General Robert E. Lee—himself celebrated before, during and after war—once captured in words the dizzying enigma of conflict: "It is well that war is so terrible; otherwise, we should grow too fond of it."

READING #9

"MY OLD KENTUCKY HOME"

AN ANALYSIS

In Louisville, every first Saturday in May at Churchill Downs, as the competing horses slowly walk to the starting gate, the whole nation becomes Kentuckians in the singing of "My Old Kentucky Home." The words nostalgically flash memories in the mind of a gentle place where "the lady" should not "weep" because remembrance of "my old Kentucky home" will support all even when "hard times comes a-knocking at our door." Abolitionist Frederick Douglass praised the power of the song, calling the composition "a heart song…[with] the finest feelings of human nature. ["My Old Kentucky Home"] can make the heart sad as well as merry, and call forth a tear as well as a smile." It should not prove surprising then that the song is often sung in praise of yet perhaps another place and another time.

Is the song really about memories of a long time ago? Or is there more to Stephen Foster's song than what the crowd believes it is?

Is the Song About Memories and Who Is the Narrator?

When looking at the lyrics in their entirety, several things become obvious. The song has a strong persona, in this case a slave, who laments that he and perhaps another will soon have to leave "my old Kentucky home." For while the "sun shines bright on my old Kentucky home," the persona is a slave who is to be sold "down river" and who realizes that the good times at his old Kentucky home will soon fade.

But for now, the other slaves are "gay" and the youngsters "roll on the cabin floor, all merry, all happy and bright." "[Yet] by'n by hard times come a-knocking at the door," meaning the slaves think that the master will have to sell some of his slaves to be able to pay his debts. The slaves then realize that very soon they will have only sweet memories to comfort them. But the slave narrator advises the lady of the cabin that she should "weep no more, my lady, weep no more today," for she too will have sweet memories to sustain her; he advises her to "sing one song for my old Kentucky home, far away."

Sold "Down South"

Is the slave narrator correct in thinking that he will soon leave "my old Kentucky home"? Exact numbers are not available, but some statistics assist in understanding just how justified the speaker is in his worry. In 1840, the state had, according to Marion Lucas's extended study of slavery in Kentucky, 182,258 slaves. By 1850, that number had shot up to 210,981 slaves, just three years before the song was published, an increase of nearly 29,000 slaves in ten years who needed shelter, clothing and food. In a word, many slave owners found themselves with far too many slaves.

Most enslaved people were concentrated in the Bluegrass Region and in the far western part of the state. In those places, slavery was more like the slavery in the Deep South, with large numbers of slaves working in hemp or tobacco fields, tending crops that called for human hands.

But for the rest of the state, such arrangements were uncommon. Unlike the large plantations of cotton, rice and sugar cane of the lower South, the "peculiar institution" in Kentucky had for the most part what may be called "domestic slavery." The slave worked directly with the master, sometimes even working beside him in planting, cultivating and harvesting crops, like smaller plots of hemp and corn, or tending farm animals, usually hogs but some sheep and cattle.

What Were Slaves' Perception of Kentucky?

The perception at the time was that life was easier for slaves in Kentucky than it was for those in the steamy and dusty cotton fields, where the slave driver was quite free with the dreadful lash of a whip if slaves did not perform to his standards. In fact, the enslaved were often literally worked to death, dying in their mid-thirties and often living in the crudest of disease-ridden cabins with only perfunctory medical care.

The loam of the once rich limestone-based soil in Kentucky lost some of its fertility, and the need for so many slaves dwindled. As a consequence, hated slave traders frequently visited farms, offering to buy excess slaves. Often, the temptation became a reality, and slave traders bought several slaves. At times, the farmer broke up whole family units, but the money farmers received for trading in human flesh frequently soothed the conscience if it could turn his "hard times" into financial gain.

The sale and delivery of slaves to the market down south was relatively easy. Some slave owners built boats large enough to accommodate fifty to seventy slaves, often chained together to prevent them from escaping. Or traders transported their human chattel on a steamboat, making the trip seem shorter, but the cost of transportation ate into the profits in the markets at Natchez, Mississippi, and New Orleans, Louisiana.

Returning from a visit to Joshua Speed near Louisville, Lincoln observed how slaves "were chained six and six together….A small clevis was around the left wrist of each, and this fastened to the main chain by a shorter one at a convenient distance from the others; so that the negroes were strung together precisely like so many fish upon a trot line." When slaves arrived at their destination, they were purchased to do hard labor for the rest of their lives in the cotton, rice or cane fields.

It was a life slaves in Kentucky had heard about and rightly dreaded.

STEPHEN FOSTER'S VIEWS OF SLAVERY

Early on, slaves were often pictured as happy and gentle people, but as Foster, the American Troubadour, more closely studied the terrible plight of southern slavery, he wrote fewer songs that portrayed them as stereotypes, like in "Old Black Joe," a composition often used in minstrel shows of the day.

But the decade of the 1850s brought real change within the nation and within Foster. In 1852, Harriet Beecher Stowe published *Uncle Tom's Cabin*, a poignant and sentimental novel that portrayed the pitiful plight of slaves in Kentucky. The story may be only legend, but President Abraham Lincoln is supposed to have said when he met Mrs. Stowe when she visited the White House, "Is this the little lady that caused this great big war?" The book had a profound effect on the nation's conscience.

Foster also felt other influences. During this same period, he spent time working as a bookkeeper in Cincinnati, across the river from slavery in Kentucky, where *Uncle Tom's Cabin* was to have taken place. But as legend has it, a visit to Judge John Rowan's estate, Federal Hill, near Bardstown, Kentucky, provided the impetus for Foster to retitle a song from "Uncle Tom," based on the character from the novel, to "My Old Kentucky Home." The story goes that Foster was inspired by the conditions of the slaves there, but little evidence exists to support that story. What seems more likely was that Foster finished the song while home near Pittsburgh, Pennsylvania.

The Second Stanza

The seldom-sung second stanza is darker than the first, with images that paint pictures of all the things the slave narrator will no longer be able to do after he is forced to leave his home:

> *They hunt no more for the 'possum and the coon,*
> *On the meadow, the hill, and the shore.*
> *They sing no more by the glimmer of the moon,*
> *On the bench by the old cabin door.*
> *The day goes by like a shadow o'er the heart,*
> *With sorrow where all was delight.*
> *The time has come when the* [slaves] *have to part,*
> *Then my old Kentucky home, good night.*

The stanza lists a number of things the narrator will miss. Typically, for example, slaves were given Sundays off from their labors. During this time, the slaves supplemented their food supply by hunting animals they could find in the immediate area. Women would forage for vegetables and roots, like poke weed, nuts and edible berries of all types. When the master butchered, he gave the slaves the parts he did not want, like the head or intestines, which the slaves turned into various dishes like souse and "chittlins."

In this same stanza, particularly poignant are the lines that refer to the slaves singing together "by the glimmer of the moon [and] on the bench by the cabin door." Slaves, then, often gathered to sing songs passed down from generation to generation by word of mouth, like "Swing Low, Sweet

Chariot," "Joshua Fit the Battle of Jericho" and "Steal Away with Jesus." The latter song became a signal to other slaves that some would try running away that night. It's not surprising that runaway slaves referred to the Ohio River as "the Jordan." When escaping slaves reached the shore of a free state, they looked for safe houses marked by various signs like a candle in a certain window or a blanket on the clothes line. Across from the bottom land in Meade County, for example, slaves who swam the Ohio River found safe houses in New Amsterdam, Indiana.

But to slaves who stayed, memories of past days of fun and frolic became "like a shadow o'er the heart" and were replaced "with sorrow where all was delight," for "the time has come when the [slaves sold to the slave trader] will have to part," and all the departed slaves will have only the remembrance of "my old Kentucky home" and the good times there to sustain them.

While in the first stanza the narrator remembers the good times, this second stanza spells out just what the slave will do.

The Third Stanza

The third stanza names what the slave "sold down river" will experience, by using three similar lines, leaving him to reflect on the memories of his home to get by:

> *The head must bow and the back will have to bend,*
> *Wherever the* [slave] *may go.*
> *A few more days and the troubles all will end.*
> *In the field where the sugar-cane may grow.*
> *A few more days for to tote the weary road,*
> *No matter 'twill never be light.*
> *A few more days till we totter on the road,*
> *Then my old Kentucky home good night.*

This stanza, like the other two, are followed by the chorus, and the narrator predicts that the long journey "will end" and "the head must bow and the back will bend...in the field where the sugar-cane may grow." The song uses the matching lines to emphasize the weary anticipation of the long journey until he arrives down south. Each line then begins with "a few more days," giving the stanza balance.

But when the slaves arrive at the destination, there "no matter 'twill never be light," with only the sweet memories of home to sustain him in the terrible life he has as a slave.

"My Old Kentucky Home" argues for the beauty of life in the Commonwealth through the words of a slave who fears being sold down south. "Hard times" have come to his master, and the narrator fears that he will be sold to the slave trader and taken away to work in dreadful conditions. The slave's words remind us all of heartfelt memories that crowd the imagination of perhaps another place and another time, but the song's melancholy melody and touching words create pictures of the good life at "my old Kentucky home."

Note: "My Old Kentucky Home" became the official state song by order of the legislature in 1928. The words were changed slightly when in 1986 *darkies* was replaced with *people*. In places, I have used *slave* when the context called for it.

READING #10

MRS. KECKLEY'S BOOK AND MRS. LINCOLN'S REACTION

It wasn't enough that she was a former slave and a woman. It wasn't enough that she was a seamstress for Mary Todd Lincoln and became her confidante and "best friend." It wasn't enough when she wrote a book, she said, to support Mrs. Lincoln in her efforts to sell her old dresses. But it was far too much when her book, *Behind the Scenes, or Thirty Years as a Slave and Four Years in the White House*, became an exposé of her "friendship" with Mrs. Lincoln.

The book had two major parts. First, it was one of many slave narratives, tracing the injustices that Mrs. Elizabeth Keckley had suffered as a slave, including her rape and subsequent life as a "sex slave." She recorded, to a degree, her indignation and harrowing experiences, including the terrible treatment by her masters and mistresses and even her half brother. While readers are told of her difficult fight to buy herself and her son, the book is a bit sketchy and limits how her readers can respond. Absent, for example, are the names of her owners. Keckley excises her owners' names because it would be "embarrassing" to her perpetrators and the punishment they inflicted.

As a slave narrative, then, the book is only ordinary, with so many competing books on the market, like *Uncle Tom's Cabin*, far surpassing Keckley's in even the basics of sentimental and alarming detail. Although most slave narratives are quite sentimental, describing the many whippings in great detail and highlighting the harsh treatment slaves received, Keckley's book suffers from a lack of details about these actions.

The second part of the book records her friendship and support of Mrs. Lincoln's emotional state, her time with the Lincoln family and reflections of the bond she had with Mrs. Lincoln. Keckley soon earned the trust of Mrs. Lincoln, who called Keckley "my best living friend." Keckley, for example, was there the night the Lincolns' infant son, Willie, died, watching over him as the Lincolns were hosting a reception at the White House. The president and first lady periodically checked in on Willie, who steadily got worse as the evening progressed and eventually passed.

Mrs. Lincoln also requested that Keckley be at her side while President Lincoln slowly succumbed to an assassin's bullet. Realizing how much Keckley meant to Mrs. Lincoln, one group frantically went to find Keckley, only to get lost in the process.

Keckley was there for the first lady's grieving process, with Mrs. Lincoln telling someone that Keckley "watched faithfully by her side." But Mary Todd Lincoln was practically inconsolable. She once summarized her state of mind: "I had an ambition to be Mrs. President; that ambition has been gratified, and now I must step down from my pedestal." To Keckley's credit, she didn't give up on the grieving widow even while others criticized the first lady for her months of grieving. To symbolize that grieving, Mrs. Lincoln wore a widow's habit the rest of her life. At the time, it seemed that nothing could break the bond between Mrs. Lincoln and Mrs. Keckley. But the publication of her book in 1868 did lasting damage to their relationship, creating a wound so deep that it would never heal.

One of Mary Lincoln's sources of contention was the publication of intimate letters between Mrs. Lincoln and Mrs. Keckley. Mrs. Keckley claimed that the publishers felt that the letters were "sensational" enough to "spice up" an otherwise dull tome. But Mrs. Keckley, in truth, had secured the letters from Mrs. Lincoln, who wanted to sow lasting doubt on Keckley's story and purpose. But Mrs. Keckley's retort was that she only wanted the public to know about Mrs. Lincoln's financial problems.

Mary Todd Lincoln's Debt Was Unknown to the President

Lincoln's assassination had another effect that Mary Lincoln hadn't planned on. Prior to the awful night at Ford's Theatre, Mrs. Lincoln had incurred a number of outstanding debts that she hadn't told her husband about, hiding the costs in the gardener's account and budget. In truth,

Lincoln himself was not in favor of the many projects that Mrs. Lincoln executed for the White House.

Lincoln himself pooh-poohed Mrs. Lincoln's attempt to redo the White House, labeling her efforts a "bunch of flubadubs [sic]," using good money, he reasoned, that could better go to the troops. But Mrs. Lincoln paid little attention and routinely exceeded the amount of money in charges at elite stores in New York and Boston. While Congress had allotted certain monies for the "freshening" of the people's house, she continued to spend vociferously and thoughtlessly in spite of Congress and her husband's efforts to stop her.

Now, after Lincoln's assassination, those bills had come due, and she was without enough money to pay the bills.

The "Old Clothes Scandal"

Congress balked at paying the bills. Realizing her fate, Mrs. Lincoln had to come up with some money-making method. She hit on the idea of selling the old dresses she had worn during her term as first lady. She imagined that many of Lincoln's admirers would jump at the chance of buying them. To assist her, she and Keckley again went to New York to find someone to mastermind the sale.

Yet the whole scheme soon leaked to the press, whose relationship with Mrs. Lincoln was tenuous at best. The press often even called her the "rebel in the White House." There were even hints in the press that she was a spy who had leaked information that would be helpful to the Confederacy.

But the sale of the old dresses went nowhere, a ploy in the end that cost money instead of earning any. Mrs. Lincoln again went back to asking Congress for more and more money, funds that Congress soon found to be unnecessary, ultimately leading to the denial of the requests. Part of Congress's reaction could be traced to her attitude.

She boasted that President Lincoln, the dead, martyred president, "saw my rich dresses and [was] happy to believe that the few hundred dollars that I obtain[ed] from him supply all my wants." At the same time, Mrs. Lincoln received some good news about her finances when she found a friend in Judge Dan Davis, who arranged for her to receive an inheritance that made the former first lady financially comfortable. In spite of the money given to Mrs. Lincoln, she designated none for Keckley to help deal with her indebtedness for material that Keckley herself had charged, expecting to be paid back. Mrs. Lincoln seemed to have forgotten her "best friend" amid her financial recovery and would not deign to give her seamstress any money.

But money wasn't the only slight Mrs. Keckley suffered. Although her book generally offered much praise of President Lincoln, when it was published, the public soon saw Mrs. Lincoln in a more focused light. The book quickly became a kind of guidebook for Mrs. Lincoln's uncontrolled disposition. In Keckley's book, Mrs. Lincoln was often portrayed as a petulant, self-centered, narcissistic person, traits that Mrs. Lincoln did not display openly to the entire world.

But Keckley's book revealed other particular instances as well. For example, the publication of intimate letters between Mrs. Lincoln and Mrs. Keckley provided the specific examples that the press knew only in part. In fact, the letters verified to the press that some of their own misgivings about the first lady were true.

Mrs. Lincoln sought answers about her suspicions of Keckley, convincing herself that she was the object of terrible cruelty. Mrs. Lincoln then saw a sinister side to the publication of the Keckley-Lincoln letters and quickly reached conclusions about Keckley's reasons for including the letters. In fact, Mrs. Lincoln remarked that she now "understood" what "evil" use the letters served. Earlier, Mrs. Lincoln called her seamstress and personal dresser one of her most intimate friends. But now Mrs. Lincoln felt betrayed, likening it to the gross insult she had received from Lincoln's law partner, William Herndon, who told Mary Todd about the Lincoln-Rutledge romance in New Salem when Lincoln was a resident there.

Feeling deeply hurt, Mrs. Lincoln called Mrs. Keckley "that colored historian." The former first lady maintained that Keckley had no right whatsoever to relate the events that transpired at the White House. Others said that Mrs. Keckley was nothing but a "gossip monger." One critic accused Mrs. Keckley of imposing herself in the everyday life of the Lincoln family, using that as a cover for the close friendship between the first lady and Keckley to gain information about the Lincolns. A reviewer even called Keckley a "treacherous creature," while another said that the lesson of the experience was that educating Black people was "a dangerous act." Keckley, a former slave at that, had described to the world what went on in the White House in her "tell-all" book. To many, it was beyond good taste.

Robert Lincoln, Mrs. Lincoln's son, convinced the publisher to halt production of the embarrassing work, but it was again published to low sales in the early 1900s.

Ardently arguing her case, Mrs. Elizabeth Keckley tried to explain that she, too, had been duped by her publisher. But it was to no avail. She tried to defend the book as a way to spur sales and alert the public of Mrs. Lincoln's financial condition. Keckley put it more gently and thought that Mrs. Lincoln "labored under pecuniary embarrassment." Apparently, Mrs. Lincoln remained very cautious of Mrs. Keckley's intentions and continued to believe that Keckley had betrayed her. The deep and abiding friendship and trust they once had had been destroyed.

Mrs. Lincoln's response to the entire relationship, whether intended or not, followed the script that Mary Todd Lincoln seems to have written for herself.

READING #11

GENERAL JOHN PALMER

WAS HE KENTUCKY'S WORST ENEMY?

When General John M. Palmer replaced General Stephen Burbridge as military commander, the *Louisville Journal* crowed, "Thank God and Mr. Lincoln!" Burbridge had been an extremely unpopular military commander, seen by many Kentuckians as "Butcher" Burbridge for executing Confederate sympathizers in retaliation for the actions of guerrillas, jailing prominent Kentuckians (including a lieutenant governor), interfering in the political processes of voting, closing the bridges to hog farmers and encouraging the enlistment of African American soldiers from Kentucky. In fact, he was so unpopular in the state that many vowed to kill him if he ever returned.

So, when General John C. Palmer assumed office as commander in Kentucky, the Commonwealth was optimistic that he would represent a break from Burbridge.

General Palmer's Military Experience

Palmer was one of those "political" generals appointed to military rank as a result of his position in his home state. Many who had been a part of Lincoln's early group of supporters found themselves in charge of Union soldiers with little or no military experience and training. Palmer was one of them.

However, he had served admirably in Missouri, but under General William T. Sherman late in the war, he became involved in a dispute with Sherman

John Palmer Used Harsh Tactics in Western Kentucky. Courtesy of Library of Congress.

over whether Palmer held rank over a West Point–trained general. Palmer argued that he was appointed earlier to his rank, but Sherman sided against him and Palmer resigned, returning home to Illinois for a short time until President Abraham Lincoln summoned him to Washington for a conference.

Lincoln Assigns Palmer to Kentucky

Lincoln told Palmer that he wanted him to assume the position Burbridge had held: "Go to Kentucky, keep your temper, do as you please, and I will sustain you." Whether Lincoln would or would not have fully endorsed just what Palmer did when he interpreted Lincoln's words may be questionable, but Palmer understood that Lincoln was very interested in dealing with their native state in a manner that would bring about the swift and sudden end of slavery in the Bluegrass State.

Earlier, Lincoln had always dealt with his birth state rather gingerly, intending to keep this very important state in the Union. "I must have

Kentucky," he once said, seeing the Commonwealth as key to keeping the loyalty of the other border states in the Union. "To lose Kentucky would be to lose the whole game," he concluded.

But by the close of the war, Lincoln had seemed intent on turning the Commonwealth in a different direction by imposing martial law, recruiting slaves for the military, imposing a series of draconian military leaders (like Burbridge) and backing away from promises he had made that Kentuckians could keep their slaves if the state stayed in the Union. Now, everything Lincoln was doing seemed to be at odds with what he had promised. Most Kentuckians were quite confused to say the least.

When Palmer assumed command on February 18, 1865, his orders came from Secretary of War Edwin Stanton. Stanton outlined Palmer's duties in a memo that included specific problems that Palmer was to tackle: rid the state of guerrillas, assist in the recruitment of "colored soldiers," "protect the property of loyal persons," see that federal law "supersedes state law in matters relating to the imprisonment of slaves seeking to enlist in military service," organize the troops in the state and promote "harmony of action and sentiment between Federal and State authorities," as Palmer noted.

In a speech accepting a welcome from the state legislature, Palmer appeared to be the kind of commander the state needed: reasonable, gracious, respectful and accommodating. Perhaps Kentucky could work with the federal government after all.

As noted in an entry in Collins's *Annals of Kentucky* for September 28, 1865, by the end of Palmer's tenure in the state, "Some of the very men who were among the foremost to welcome and cajole the petty tyrant, General John M. Palmer, when he made his advent in Kentucky as the successor of General Burbridge, are now willing to see the latter reinstated in preference." What had Palmer done to incite such comments? After all, Palmer had followed one of the most hated men in Kentucky in the person of General Stephen Burbridge. How in such a short time had Palmer elicited such condemnation from people in the Commonwealth?

Where Did Palmer Go Wrong?

Palmer appeared to have crossed the line in the minds of many Kentuckians in a number of different areas. When Palmer went to Kentucky, he said, "I made up my mind that all that was left of slavery was its mischiefs, and that I would encourage a system of gradual emancipation, a thing that has been desired so long, and which the colored people had pretty well established for themselves." Had Palmer interpreted Lincoln's words to mean that Palmer was to end slavery in Kentucky? Was that what Lincoln had ordered Palmer to do? Historian George Wright argued that slavery was already dead in Kentucky long before Palmer ever arrived. He maintains that the signs of the disintegration of slavery as a viable institution in the Commonwealth emanated "from the beginning of the Civil War" and that "Kentucky slaves were active participants in the drama. From the moment Northern troops entered Kentucky, the objective of slaves was to secure more self-determinism for themselves and their families." Wright noted that the enslaved quickly figured out that the Union army provided, in some instances, the path to freedom, employing many slaves and sheltering them from masters who supported the Confederacy.

Enslaved people also firmly believed that their time had come: the long-awaited "jubilee" had arrived and the shackles would soon fall from their necks. Adding to that, when Confederate forces invaded the state in the late summer and fall of 1862, some masters fled to the protection of the Union army, leaving many slaves on their own. Slave owners that held Southern sympathies ran south, also leaving their slaves unattended.

What resulted was a large number of slaves free to find their own employment or demand from their masters pay for their work performed. While state law forbad slaves from seeking their own work and the state responded by imprisoning large numbers of slaves, the situation was far from stable for the slave owners.

One provision of the Emancipation Proclamation was the enlistment of Black soldiers into the military, providing still another way for slaves to free themselves. According to Lincoln, Kentucky was supposed to be initially exempt from Black troops being stationed in the state, and although slaves were only supposed to be eligible for enlistment with the permission of their masters, slaves soon learned how to circumvent that problem. But runaway slaves in Louisville became pawns and often were sold as "substitutes" for White soldiers until the practice was outlawed.

Slaves joining the military was a problem for many Whites, who were being confronted with being drafted into the Union army; in Madison County, a number of slave owners from there asked that "said persons be enlisted as soldiers in the United States Service, [and] that the County have the proper credit [for the enlistment quota]." Wright also pointed out that attempts even by Palmer to encourage the runaway slaves to return to their original masters and work for pay was a plan that felt too much like a return to slavery to almost all Blacks. In fact, Wright concluded that as early as 1863, "slavery ceased to be a viable institution in Kentucky long before the Thirteenth Amendment [to outlaw slavery] was adopted."

Even Civil War veteran and Kentucky governor at the time Thomas Bramlette observed that slavery was a dying if not dead institution in the state and encouraged the state to ratify the Thirteenth Amendment, but the state maintained its stubborn stance that slavery was a right guaranteed by state law, in spite of what the federal government said or did.

As a federal officer and military commander in Kentucky, Palmer soon became a clear target for criticism, despite circumstances that made it clear that slavery in Kentucky was gasping for its last breath. Instead, Palmer became the problem.

Despite the State of Slavery, Palmer Goes Ahead

Palmer himself, in the eyes of stubborn slave owners, did not help his cause by his actions in Louisville on July 4, 1865, more than two months after Appomattox, the surrender that was to end the war.

Word had spread among Black residents that at a celebration in Louisville Palmer was going to free all slaves in Kentucky. Slaves from all over the state flocked to the Derby City for the momentous announcement. Palmer had been forewarned that the rumors had been flying for weeks and denied that he planned to take such actions, even while Blacks were convinced that this was their day of reckoning. Nonetheless, Palmer chose to enter the scene in front of an expectant and jubilant Black crowd on a golden chariot with two piebald horses borrowed from a circus owner. One enslaved person, overcome with emotion, shouted, "Dar he comes in a golden chariot and the hosses of salvation!" Lifted by the crowd to the speaker's stand, Palmer declared, "My countrymen, you are substantially free." Realizing that the crowd's interpretation was quite different from what he meant, Palmer revised what the said and acquiesced to the crowd's wishes: "My countrymen, you are free, and while I command in the department the military forces of the United States will defend your right to freedom." The problem with the Whites in the state was that what Palmer had said was in direct opposition with state law that permitted slavery (and would until the enactment of the Thirteenth Amendment some six month later). Palmer, the Whites in Kentucky thought, was supplanting state law with federal military rule, a sore already festering in the minds of many White Kentuckians.

Palmer was already at odds with state officials over the issuances of passes to Blacks to travel and work wherever they pleased. In Palmer's defense, he argued that the passes were issued at the request of Louisville city officials to prevent the vagrancy that existed in the city with the influx of so many Black people. But charges soon flew abroad that Palmer issued these passes less as a way to control crowds and more as a way to speed up the emancipation process.

Merton Coulter's detailed history of the period notes that Palmer "began by giving passes to the wives and children of negro soldiers and to other free negroes, but he soon speeded up the milling mass of blacks by issuing passes to all comers," a perception that reinforced the idea that Palmer himself would eliminate slavery in Kentucky, despite state laws that cruelly hung on to the institution, no matter how immoral and dead it was.

State law said that slavery was legal in Kentucky, Whites argued, and the federal government had no business interfering in the state's "institutions."

Governor Thomas Bramlette Asks Palmer for Help

Besides imposing federal policy on its citizens, speeding up the emancipation of slaves and the issuance of "Palmer passes," General Palmer was also guilty of meddling in the voting process across that state, or so his critics alleged.

In late summer elections of 1865, the populace was to vote for a slate of candidates that represented both ends of the political spectrum—some who favored the federal government's policies and some conservatives who bitterly opposed the federal control in the state. Governor Thomas Bramlette realized that the election would be a mandate over where the state was headed in the next few years, and he and his backers campaigned for candidates favorable to ratification of the Thirteenth Amendment and other measures that he felt would put the state on the road to economic recovery and finally put the war behind them.

One of Bramlette's greatest fears was that the election would become an opportunity for those who had served or were Southern in their sympathies during the war to grab power. To prevent those people from voting and swaying the election toward a more conservative position, he asked General Palmer to assist him in disqualifying those attempting to vote who were ineligible either by law or due to their sympathy with the Southern cause.

But Bramlette did not accurately predict the consequences of his request. Palmer responded to Bramlette's request by issuing orders for the military to supervise the election process across the state, sometimes using Black soldiers to do so. While overall, the conservatives were winners in the election, there were still charges that the military had grossly interfered in the voting process in a number of different polling places and wrongly disqualified voters on the slimmest of grounds.

Coulter, for example, noted that "the military authorities had acted outrageously; they had assumed control of the election, as if they were wholly an affair of the army, and had assumed to decide who should vote and who should not." According to some observers, some were disqualified from voting simply because of their opposition to the Thirteenth Amendment.

Opposition to Palmer's tactics flew even from the North. The *Cincinnati Commercial* noted that "it is not becoming that a file of soldiers shall stand before the polls, and that the officers of the army of the United States shall hold lists of those proscribed, made out by irresponsible persons, and prevent them from approaching the ballot box." Other newspapers across the North echoed the Cincinnati paper's observation.

In some cases, the military interference was so blatant that the results were nullified, and elections were held at a later date to determine just who the legitimate winner was.

Palmer's Undoing

Both Bramlette and ardent unionist Green Clay tried to "get rid of Palmer," as historian Coulter noted, but even General William T. Sherman, an old rival with great influence, couldn't secure the immediate removal of Palmer. Yet Sherman's stance on Palmer was quite unequivocal: "[If it were] monarchy or consolidation we are after, he is right; but if we want to preserve the old form of government, he is all wrong." In addition to the most obvious charges against him, Palmer also faced a number of lawsuits brought against him by prominent Kentuckians as a consequence of his actions to free slaves. Although he notified the adjutant general of his wish to resign on February 19, 1866, he remained in office until March to fight the court proceedings that eventually led to his exoneration.

There is little doubt that Palmer's motive to rid the state of the evils of slavery was pure and noble. Defense of the institution of slavery in Kentucky at the time was not only fruitless but grossly immoral, yet the White citizens of Kentucky were determined to hang on to at least the appearance of slavery until the very end. Palmer was, to them, an all-too-clear reminder of the power of the federal government at a time when many Kentuckians felt that the federal government had grossly mistreated the Bluegrass State, despite its remaining in the Union.

Palmer returned to Illinois, was elected governor and later U.S. senator and ran for president, changing political parties several times before dying on September 25, 1900. He was no doubt a man of great passion and firm belief, rooted in decisive action. But to the White citizens of Kentucky, he had gone too far too fast. In the end, history will judge whether the citizens of the Commonwealth were right.

READING #12

THE SLAUGHTER AT SIMPSONVILLE

A MASSACRE TOO LONG FORGOTTEN?

OTHER MASSACRES

Atrocities occur in almost all wars. They are expected, but they are not generally excused. When mostly men are trained to kill or capture or maim the enemy, a tiny segment of soldiers may take this information and mindset and go too far and inflict injury on innocent people.

That is not to excuse the actions of the few who murder or maim noncombatants and who then call such incidents legitimate acts of war. Massacres are perpetrated by a few of those who are trained for war but who, unlike the vast majority, cross the line and kill innocent people. Confederate General Nathan Bedford Forrest said it this way: "War is killing." That is true, but it is not indiscriminant killing.

One relatively recent example of crossing the line is the murder of innocent civilians—old men, women and children—by Charlie Company at My Lai on March 16, 1968, during the Vietnam War. The confusion over just what soldiers were responsible and how they would be punished ignited a considerable amount of antiwar sentiment as the nation searched its conscience for answers.

Occurring on November 29, 1864, during the Civil War years, the slaughter of innocent American Indians near Sand Creek, Colorado, stemmed from an unclear order from commanders that resulted in out-of-control soldiers whose hatred of all Indians prompted a massacre of men, women and children. The commanding officer, Colonel John M. Chivington, later met stinging criticism from even Madison County–born Kit Carson,

Slavery Was Immoral. *Courtesy of Library of Congress.*

who spoke of the incident: "[Chivington's] men shot down squaws, and blew the brains out of innocent children. You call sich [*sic*] soldiers Christians, do ye?...I never yet drew a bead on a squaw or papoose, and I despise the man who would." Explanations of the troops' acts were legion, but clearly those in Washington thought that Chivington and his men had crossed a line between war and slaughter.

According to many, during the course of the conflict, the Civil War itself was not without accusations of such atrocities.

Civil War Massacres

The most famous incident was the April 12, 1864 action of Confederate soldiers at the Battle of Fort Pillow, at the time a Union installation upstream from Memphis, Tennessee. Some observers say that soldiers under Major General Nathan Bedford Forrest slaughtered Yankee White and Black soldiers who had raised their hands, pleading to surrender, but were killed anyway. Forrest, who was not present at the storming of the fort, was not completely exonerated, but his men were roundly criticized by both Union and Confederate commanders for their barbarity.

More recent scholarship uncovered one of the most egregious examples of the slaughter of unarmed soldiers during the course of the war. It happened at Saltville, Virginia, during the first few days of October in 1864. After being roundly defeated, Union forces under General Stephen Burbridge hurriedly left wounded men on the field and in a local hospital. While several Confederate irregulars participated, the blame was assigned in large part to Confederate guerrilla Champ Ferguson, who after the battle was accused of summarily shooting wounded Yankees on the field and in the hospital. Ferguson was said to be especially angered by the presence of Black soldiers.

After the war, his trial for war crimes revealed Ferguson to be an untamed killer rather than a legitimate soldier. Brian McKnight's book on Ferguson noted that it was Ferguson's "habit during the earliest days of the war [to] certainly participate…in the killings," but, as McKnight concluded, others also engaged in the slaughter at Saltville. As scholarship grows, the account of the massacre details the extent of the slaughter.

Massacres Not Noted

One massacre has escaped much of the attention given to these other incidents. Unlike most other atrocities, with their complicated explanations and extensive justifications, the events suggest that the name "Slaughter at Simpsonville" seems particularly apt to describe just what happened outside this small central Kentucky town.

At the time, news reports were quite confused about just who the guerrillas were and assigned leadership of the gang of marauding Confederate guerrillas to different individuals. Some said that the gang's commander was Isaiah Coulter, some said Henry Magruder and still others said Dick Taylor—all notorious guerrilla leaders.

While good journalistic practices should have ferreted out just who the leader was, in view of the extent of guerrilla activity in the state, the confusion is understandable, especially when eyewitness accounts themselves were unclear and differed considerably.

In fact, the everyday experience of most Kentuckians at the time was to have their own community assaulted by roving bands of ex-Confederate and Union soldiers. Since most guerrillas had left legitimate Union and Confederate units, they then had "gone out on their own," robbing and pillaging even those who held Union and Confederate sympathies. Sometimes they stole horses, robbed banks or sought to exact revenge on a particular victim. In many ways, these same guerrillas may have at one time have had legitimate sympathies with either the Confederate or Union causes, but they adopted instead some sort of freelance approach to fighting the war that was outside the usual commands.

The most famous guerrilla was a long-haired, swashbuckling young man from Todd County, Marcellus Jerome Clarke, whose youth and mane labelled him as "Sue Mundy." He was ultimately captured in a barn in Meade County and, after a short trial, hanged. Others knew of Henry Magruder, another famous guerrilla whose reputation for senseless mayhem preceded him wherever he went. Although the names of many guerrillas have been forgotten, the reputations of some were quite familiar to most Kentuckians at the time.

As a result, not knowing the leader of this gang would be expected, with so many guerrillas actively engaged in every kind of illegal operation in so many places across the Commonwealth.

Camp Nelson as a Training Facility

Originally, Camp Nelson in rural Jessamine County was a supply depot, but it became a training facility for Black soldiers. The military base then grew rapidly when Black troops were recruited as fighting men in the middle of the war after the issuance of the Emancipation Proclamation on January 1, 1863.

According to the Kentucky Heritage Council, the base covered more than four thousand acres and boarded some fourteen thousand horses and mules but still remained "a major supply depot…that supported Union campaigns in Tennessee, Georgia and Virginia." The population of the camp quickly grew, and it trained more than ten thousand Black soldiers, the third-largest training facility in the nation. Along the borders of the camp grew a kind of "shantytown" as soldiers brought their wives and children to be close to them. Schools, churches, warehouses, livestock pens and barns and even hospitals quickly opened to serve not only the men but also their families.

The Massacre Itself

Feeding the soldiers alone required an enormous amount of food. To provide enough meat to feed the soldiers, in December 1864, commander of the installation Union General Stephen Burbridge sent some noncommissioned White men and a White officer, Lieutenant Augustus Flint, to lead some eighty members of the 5th U.S. Colored Cavalry, a Black contingent from various companies, to herd between nine hundred and one thousand cattle to Louisville to provide meat for troops back at Camp Nelson. (At the time, Black soldiers had to be led by White officers.) In the bitter cold, by January 25, 1865, without any difficulty, the body of cattle and soldiers neared Simpsonville, Kentucky, just south of Louisville. At that point, the commander, Lieutenant Flint, left and went to Simpsonville to buy boots and to warm himself, with plans to catch up with his soldiers later in the day.

Guerrilla fighters were in the area, and scouts soon made the guerrillas aware of the presence of the Union forces. Truly, it was a target the guerrillas could not resist. All of a sudden, a body of fifteen Confederate guerrillas attacked the Union soldiers from the rear, emptying their guns on the hapless group of Black recruits and frightening the cattle, which fled in all directions. The Black soldiers attempted to surrender; as historian Berry Craig noted, because the cold rain followed by light snow affected the powder in their guns, their firearms were rendered useless.

The guerrillas ignored the soldiers' pleas for surrender, while "yelling like devils" and shooting the Union soldiers indiscriminately. The other soldiers in the lead did attempt to fire back at the guerrillas, but the Union soldiers were unable to get off even one shot. After the attack was over, twenty-two Black soldiers had been killed and eight were critically wounded. One source says that four of the wounded later died. The bodies of those who died at Simpsonville were all buried in an unmarked mass grave. The location is still a mystery.

Lieutenant Flint, according to one account, "heard of the attack, and cowered in the basement of the dry goods store in Simpsonville, planning his escape." Another source added that Flint stayed hidden until he was sure that the guerrillas were gone.

But there are indications that Flint was in deep trouble over his conduct during the slaughter of troops. Brigadier General Hugh Ewing openly worried about the leadership or the lack of leadership, asking investigators to "ascertain if any officers were in command of the guard; if so, arrest and bring them to these headquarters. Give this matter your immediate attention and report the department [to me]." Ewing also called attention to the medical staff of the slaughter and sent troops to round up the cattle, "to collect them and drive them to [Shelbyville]." When he learned of the massacre, Brigadier General E.H. Hobson in nearby Lexington at the time also asked that mounted soldiers be sent "to get to them" as soon as possible. But help was late in coming.

After the slaughter, these same guerrillas returned to Simpsonville to boast of their accomplishments; as the plaque at the site marking the massacre notes, "The killers seemed perfectly delighted with what they had accomplished."

Why Simpsonville Qualifies as a Massacre

This little-known massacre of Union troops qualifies as a slaughter, but the actions of the guerrillas are not easily explained. Were the guerrillas prompted by the sight of virtually unarmed Black soldiers and found it an opportune time to express their anger at seeing Black men wearing Union uniforms? To the guerrillas, the Black soldiers should not even be free much less soldiers.

Or did the guerrillas see the Yankee soldiers as driving cattle to market for feeding Union troops and therefore justify their actions? Clearly, though, the guerrillas would have quickly realized that because the Union soldiers were unable to fire a shot at them, the guerrillas were not engaged in legitimate act of war. In truth, the guerrillas themselves were not even legitimate Confederate soldiers and therefore could not be even engaged in any legitimate act of war. They had left those Confederate armies to freelance for themselves, honoring no rules, except those that ensured their own survival. An attack of any kind from this group of freelance soldiers was not then an act of war at all, because as guerrillas it was their own choice where and when they were to pillage and plunder. They obeyed no chain of command from any commander of legitimate forces.

Guerrillas were free to conduct themselves in any way they saw fit, inflicting their brand of bullying havoc on anyone they chose, friend or foe. In their minds, determining whether someone was their enemy was not a studied and deliberate process; often they decided in the heat of unreasoned passion.

Guerrillas operated on rumors, not facts, deciding when and where they would bring violence to a particular place, at a specific time, to a particular individual. As Gerald W. Fischer makes plain in his *Guerrilla Warfare in the Civil War in Kentucky*, guerrilla warfare was quite extensive in most parts of the Commonwealth—they were ultimately out of control.

In truth, Confederate General Robert E. Lee knew that if the Confederacy wanted, the whole war could be extended by resorting to guerrilla warfare, but he rightly rejected such a move, realizing that an honorable surrender was the only way to begin the necessary healing process. In point of fact, a few guerrillas did continue their mayhem even after the Confederate surrender.

What happened at Simpsonville curdles even the most generous milk of human kindness. The real shame, though, is that it has lain forgotten for far too long; it deserves a place in any discussion of atrocities committed during the Civil War. It reminds us that even checked by some sort of system of "just war," atrocities like those at Simpsonville can still happen.

My thanks to Robert Bell for his help with this reading.

READING #13

THE EXPULSION AT CAMP NELSON AND THE EMANCIPATION PROCLAMATION

In April 1864, having slaves in Kentucky after the issuance of Lincoln's Emancipation Proclamation on January 1, 1863, presented a difficult problem for both slave owners and slaves. Should the masters allow their slaves to leave their "homes?" Or should slave owners permit male slaves of an appropriate age to leave the master's supervision? Lincoln's proclamation, according to many people then and now, was mistakenly seen as freeing *all* slaves everywhere. It did not. The slaves in the states in "rebellion" were entirely free. These were slaves in the states that had formally seceded from the Union.

But slaves in border states until April 1864 (Kentucky, Missouri, Maryland and Delaware) were not free, except for those covered in another whole part of the amended document dealing with "colored soldiers." As of January 1, 1863, a woman and her children were not free in the border states.

In fact, important exemptions later existed for other slaves in the border states in the Proclamation with the amendments of April 1864. That is to say, male slaves of the right age, even in the border states, in April 1864, were given an important option now covered in the document.

Lincoln saw the Emancipation Proclamation as a "war measure" because the president said that he could not rid the entire country of slavery as president for several reasons. First, he recognized the party platform he was elected on was one impediment to abolishing slavery in all the states. He had promised not to touch slavery where it "already existed." At the time, preserving the Union was the war's goal. But as a war strategy, Lincoln could

Men in a Civil War Prison Camp. *Courtesy of Library of Congress.*

deprive those slave owners in the Confederacy of the labors of their slaves. In fact, many slaves of the Confederacy were used to build and repair bridges and make fortresses that would provide safety for Confederate soldiers. Lincoln saw such projects as war-related.

The second reason he couldn't free all the slaves everyplace was that the Constitution itself permitted or strongly implied that slavery was legal where it already existed. While the wording was unclear, the Constitution was seen as permitting slavery as a part of the defense of private property clauses in the document.

Third, to allay fears of blanketly freeing all slaves everywhere, Lincoln also said in his first inaugural address that he wouldn't bother slavery in the border states where it already occurred, hoping that his words would dissuade the southern states from seceding from the Union.

But the people of the Confederacy had made up their minds and saw Lincoln as intent on destroying slavery. Even the vice president of the Confederacy, Alexander Hamilton Stephens, saw the South as a "slaveocracy," dependent on slavery to keep its economy running.

But Lincoln was specific: "I have no purpose, directly or indirectly, to interfere with the institution of slavery in the States where it exists." Slaves in say, Mississippi, male or female, young and old, were entirely free as a result of the Emancipation Proclamation because Mississippi was one of the states in rebellion. Another section of the same document covered those males of an appropriate age from the states in rebellion. That section established "colored soldiers" as a fighting unit in the Union army, but the men were led then by White officers.

In April 1864, the conditions changed for border slave states, including Kentucky. The edict said that if an appropriately aged male slave from Kentucky or any other border state wanted his freedom, then he must become a soldier. He would then leave with his master's permission to join his constituents in the "colored troops."

As expected, many Kentucky slaves of a suitable age and gender gained their freedom to join the soldiers, for they were anxious to participate in the war. In fact, when the number of Black soldiers were all counted, more ex-slaves from Kentucky joined up than any other state except Louisiana. Kentucky slaves and their families, along with other border states, with or without their master's permission, flocked to Camp Nelson.

Yet while an appropriately aged enslaved man from Kentucky could gain his freedom according to this document and its amendments, his wife and children would not be free and would continue as property of the slave owner. Therefore, if an eligible male did *not* volunteer for the "colored troops," he, according to the Emancipation Proclamation and later additions, also was not free. Until April 1864, any eligible male in the border states could gain his freedom if he joined the "colored troops."

As commander in chief, Lincoln had the authority to render the Emancipation Proclamation as a "necessary military measure" applicable only to the states in rebellion. Lincoln later worried that since the Emancipation Proclamation was only a war measure, it could lose its effect after the war was over. As a consequence, later in his administration, he campaigned heavily to pass what became the Thirteenth Amendment to the Constitution to free slaves in the entire country, but an assassin's bullet denied Lincoln the chance to see the ratification of the Thirteenth Amendment.

Ex-Slaves Have Their Reservations

Many soldiers worried about the treatment of the remaining wives and children. Ostensibly, the masters of the women and children could retaliate for the loss of their husbands and fathers to the "colored troops." Several masters did, in fact, mistreat the families of men who had so volunteered, retaliating by not feeding the slaves, by tearing down their shacks, by beating them and ultimately by expelling them from the farms.

Consequently, a sizeable number of women and children escaped and fled to their husbands at Camp Nelson, near Nicholasville, where many other "colored soldiers" were receiving training. The "refugee" women occupied ground next to Camp Nelson in an array of shacks, tents and other temporary buildings, hoping to survive by doing laundry and baking pies and cakes for the soldiers in training at Camp Nelson—doing anything to survive.

General Speed Fry, the Commander at Camp Nelson

The man in charge of Camp Nelson was Brigadier General Speed Smith Fry, a White Boyle County native who felt little compassion for the women and children occupying the fringes of the camp in temporary structures.

First, Fry sent many slaves back to their masters, assuming that the masters wanted them. Second, on July 6, 1864, Fry telegraphed a commanding officer, asking for an order to rid the camp of women and children "unfit for the service [who] will be delivered to their masters." According to Richard Sears's *Camp Nelson*, General Fry did receive the order in a telegram later that same day. The military authorities, however, later said that the order was not to be followed, that the order was indeed "bogus." The existence of such an order, then, was a question that really never quite got settled for Fry and his underlings.

Fry thought that he had military orders, so he ordered his troops to harass the children and women in the camp. In truth, part of the problem was the army's ambiguous notion of what to do with "refugees." Historian Patrick O'Neil explained that the army did not have a well-stated policy on such refugees and that "the presence of these women and children in the camp posed problems for army officials." Finally, by November 26, 1864, Fry had had enough. He had been patient, he thought, for he had delayed action for months.

With the weather bitterly cold and snowy, four hundred women and children were forcibly expelled from the environs of Camp Nelson. One guard under Fry is said to have told the wife of Private John Higgins when she protested that she was sick, "If you do not get out we will burn the house over your heads." The women and children did leave—some to a mission house on the route. Some were found in barns, some were found in mule sheds, some were found "languishing along the way" and some were wandering aimlessly in the woods. All were destitute, helpless and cold women and children with literally no place to go. Of the 400 hundred women and children forced out of Camp Nelson, 102 persons died, either from sickness or the cold weather.

Captain Theron E. Hall strongly objected to Fry's order at the time of the expulsion—so much so that Fry slapped a court-martial for insubordination on Captain Hall. When Stephen Burbridge, commanding general for the state of Kentucky, learned of Fry's order, he ordered Fry "not [to] expel any more Negro women and children from Camp Nelson." At the same time, Burbridge issued orders that Fry was to "give quarters and if necessary erect buildings for them and allow back all who have been turned out." Burbridge then countermanded Fry's call for a court-martial for Captain Hall and ordered Hall to superintend the construction of the buildings for the "refugees." When outside sources heard what happened at Camp Nelson, newspapers called Fry's actions "deliberate depravity and cool malignity." The press also asked questions about the Union army's creation and treatment of "colored troops."

What happened to the women and children at Camp Nelson hastened the end of the Civil War and, in part, changed slavery into a very real moral issue, dealing with real women and real children. The slave owners in Kentucky were thus faced with perplexing questions: Should they try to recapture the women and children who left bondage to be with their husbands at Camp Nelson? Would the slave owners continue to hold the women and children who were slaves as their "property"? It was a dilemma that would soon have epic conclusions—a new day was coming.

READING #14

IF THE SOUTH HAD WON THE WAR

The study of history has a way of asking questions about what would happen if things had gone differently. What if, for example, the British had won the Revolutionary War? After all, the British army was large and well trained and should have won that war against a poorly trained and rather small army like the Continentals. How would life in a British colony be different? Would we speak differently? Would our cultural values be more like those in England? Yet while speculation is a fun game, the reality is that such events did not really happen.

In a different war, the Civil War, what if the Confederate States of America had won some key battles? By early 1863, the Confederates, particularly under Lee, were very close to total victory. Lincoln knew it, and the Confederacy knew it too. In fact, Lincoln told his cabinet that they should prepare for a change in guard, perhaps a government quite different from the one already ensconced in Washington, D.C.

What then, if the Union was so tired of war, as it surely was, led to the election of former general George McClellan as president if he, like many of his countrymen, would have admitted that the South had won the war? Would his administration be willing to sit down with the South and arrange a lasting peace? McClellan would have had to recognize the Confederacy as a separate and sovereign country worthy of recognition. After all, the South had defeated the Union in a series of crucial battles, like First and Second Manassas, Chancellorsville and Fredericksburg. In addition, Jubal Early and his fellow Southerners in a daring raid could have captured Washington, D.C., and, more importantly, the White House, taking Lincoln, his wife and family along with important cabinet members like Secretary of State William Seward and Treasury Secretary Salmon Chase. How would the South treat its captors? How different would life in the two countries be if the South had won the war? Remember that Lincoln vowed in his early speeches that he would not bother slavery where it "already existed." But the South went to war because it wanted to acquire new land, and the Republican platform on which Lincoln was elected wouldn't specifically forbid it in states where it did not already exist. Slavery would surely continue for a number of years, for South Carolina and fellow members of the Confederacy believed that an abolitionist like Lincoln would hasten the collapse of the southern paternal plantation system. Lincoln was a known liar after all. "Slaveocracy," Confederate vice president Alexander Stephens said, was at the foundation of southern life and economy, but the South needed more land to prosper. The South, in fact, was a largely an agricultural region, with cotton as king and other crops like indigo and rice also a part of the agricultural mix.

Would the South have looked at territories like Nebraska and Kansas as possible places cotton could be grown? Would California and New Mexico, where cotton is also grown, join the ranks of other cotton-growing states and look to the Confederacy as the most likely country to align themselves with? The South would, in turn, look at other unsettled territories in the West and Midwest as being open to becoming a part of the Confederacy.

Or would the Midwest take a cue from the South and instead secede from the Union, reasoning that its own agricultural industry was vigorous enough to support a separate country? Just how far would the secession movement go? The size of present-day United States is large enough to be divided into several countries—see Europe for an example.

California and Texas had already been countries separate from the United States. Would they want to retain that status? Would Texans see as foolish the move they made to join the United States? Texas covers much territory, with a climate and topography suited for all kinds of agriculture. When added together with West Texas, the whole state was made up of mostly arable land, enough land to feed its citizens. Texas, too, was large enough to support myriad industries and presumably meet the needs of its residents. Since there were slaves there and since many of the early settlers were from the South, Texas probably would continue to have slaves, especially if it continued its emphasis on agriculture as its major commodity.

More particularly, what if Confederate General Robert E. Lee had not made the mistakes he made and actually handily won the Battle of Gettysburg? What if, undercover, Grant had been assassinated outside Vicksburg by a deranged soldier and his troops had lost the will to open up the Mississippi at Vicksburg as their fallen leader wanted? The "Glorious Fourth" that the Union so celebrated, with victories at Gettysburg and Vicksburg, would have been instead a dark day for the Union, faced with growing disillusionment with the war in most of the Union. After all, many see those two victories as key to the Union's winning the war, but by this time, the North citizenry would really have been frustrated by the defeats. Would Confederate General John Bell's diversion tactic to lure General William T. Sherman's troops toward Kentucky into a death trap somewhere outside Nashville negate the Christmas message that Lincoln would not receive? Would the guerrilla troops and the other partisan rangers cease their raids in the border regions and join in peaceful coexistence with their fellow southerners? In reality, Union troops spent much of their time and energy chasing after these warriors. The success of the Union troops combating these groups had brought little success and a lot of bad feelings among the citizens. Dictatorial generals like Generals Stephen Burbridge and John Palmer had done much to excite passions against the Union.

In Kentucky, the whole state was near rebellion. Is it possible that everyday Kentucky citizens would finally rebel against such draconian leaders the Union had appointed? Would Kentucky, already very disappointed with the "antics" of the Lincoln administration and its attempts to "end slavery" in the Commonwealth, be more comfortable as southerners? Would its citizens see the Confederacy as the natural place it wanted to be a part of? After all, Kentucky did have slaves and wanted to keep them, but many White Kentuckians were convinced that the Civil War would free the slaves Kentucky so needed. To them, the Emancipation Proclamation was not a "military measure" but a ploy by Lincoln to redefine the Civil War's goals and abolish slavery. As a result, many Kentuckians felt their values, culture and institutions were more in line with the Confederacy. In other words, was the state like historian Merton Coulter observed, a state that would join the Confederacy after the war? Many Kentucky citizens practiced agriculture like much of the South, where growing cotton was the major crop. Kentucky did have essential crops like tobacco and hemp that depended on slaves. Kentucky, too, like much of the South, had an agricultural-based economy. To that end, its citizens believed that they needed slavery in order to survive and keep the economic engine running smoothly. That meant that slave labor would likely continue in both Kentucky and the rest of the South for as long as the regions had agricultural economies based on the labor of slaves.

Would the Bluegrass State be able to attract industry as it had in cities like Louisville that would help keep the southern way of life possible? The Confederate states would most likely count on the coal production in eastern Tennessee and Kentucky and parts of Virginia to provide enough coal to be the foundation of industry the South obviously desired and needed. For example, would the Confederacy build the necessary railroads out of coal country to supply the industries in the upper South where southern industry had spouted up in places like Louisville? Would Kentucky still be known as a source for horses? After all, horses were essential to the lives of millions of people in both the North and the South. Horses can come from many parts of the world, but none seem to compare with the horses from Kentucky, many people felt. Would flocks of buyers from the North show up at horse sales eager to buy quality animals? Or would the North look to other places for quality horseflesh?

Traditionally, the wars of the United States since the Civil War attracted many southerners, filling out the muster roles. Would the South have sided with the North in these wars and continued the tradition of strong support for wars? Or would the South take a more independent path than the North and see the wars as something it wanted no part of? Would Southerners side with Great Britain, conscious that the cotton the South provided the British textile mills would ultimately decide just what side the South was on? Would Confederates be eager to join with the Union in other matters of foreign policy? Or would the Confederacy become more isolationistic in its foreign policy, seeing the Union, perhaps, as colleagues but not necessarily be in lockstep with their thinking and ways? Perhaps the South would be just the opposite and involve itself in *more* wars than the North would support? The South, as it had been from President James Polk forward, saw Cuba as desirable territory that would be valuable not only for its sugar production but also as an area rich in natural resources that could aid the economic needs of the Confederacy. The South perhaps would go to war over Cuba, annex it and see the island as a source of sugar as well as other necessities of Southern life.

These and other questions would need to be settled by a government like the North's, but with the constitutional emphasis on states' rights, a right so dear to its citizens. The South had the advantage of several good generals—Robert E. Lee and "Stonewall" Jackson come to mind—and too often the North's "political" generals brought death and destruction to the battlefield because of their bungling ways.

Would a war of attrition, like that of Grant and other Union generals, be overcome by Confederate forces in decisive victories, avoiding the bloodbaths like Cold Harbor, where such a practice seemed to be the obvious tactic? Obviously, we will never know, but we can harmlessly speculate about it.

CONCLUSION

The Thirteenth Amendment, in spite of Kentucky's unwillingness at the time to ratify the amendment, eliminated slavery from American society. Has Kentucky accepted former slaves and their descendants on an equal basis with most of the White population? As the readings indicate, some White Kentucky citizens at one time fought very hard to cite legal arguments to defend the institution of slavery, seeing slavery as a matter of property and supported by the words of the federal Constitution. But more importantly, Kentuckians felt that Lincoln would not interfere with the practice as long as the state was loyal to the Union. Some would argue that the state sided with the Union for that very purpose, thinking that as long as the state supported the Union it could keep its slaves, even after the war itself. Kentuckians believed fervently that they had a lawful right to retrieve their own slaves as "fugitives" in the Northern states. After all, it was then possible, in spite of the Emancipation Proclamation, to be a slave owner *and* still fight to preserve the Union.

Indeed, it was not a surprise to loyal Kentuckians when the war became a war to free the slaves rather than a war to preserve the Union. They had suspected it for a long time. In fact, when Kentuckians realized that the war had another purpose, the Commonwealth aligned itself more with the South, an action after a series of "slights" by the Lincoln administration, like the appointments of several military governors like Stephen G. Burbridge and E.A. Paine who seemed to enrage citizens with their approach to governing the citizens of the Commonwealth.

Conclusion

In the Union, those who supported the abolition of slavery kept alive their dreams of freedom when people in Union states resisted the Fugitive Slave Law. The president's wife also seemed quite content with her seemingly undying friendship with a former slave, giving hope to slaves that Whites and Blacks could get along. The humanitarian aid given to the Camp Nelson women and children who had been expelled from the camp seemed to hasten the freedom movement in the state. Yet most of all, the work of General John Palmer in Louisville heightened the anticipation that slaves would soon be free.

A word of caution, though. Even if the South had won the war, as many thought would happen, Kentucky likely would join the Confederacy, and the slaves' vision of freedom would never become anything but a mirage. The dream of White power seems to have not died, if we are as realistic as speculation permits us.

The South winning the war, of course, did not become a reality. Sadly, though, in the Commonwealth, even after other states had ratified the Thirteenth Amendment, many Whites could not accept these freed slaves as equal citizens. True, the conditions of Black citizens in the state are somewhat better because the federal laws of the 1960s changed not just Kentucky but the entire nation, but many White citizens in the state still regard Black people as inferior.

Wendell Berry, a famous Kentucky writer, wrote about slavery and its heritage within the state. Berry called his book *The Hidden Wound*, a metaphorical reference to a hidden wound that will not heal until the state has acknowledged the effect that slavery has had on the Commonwealth and the subsequent years since slavery—the open sore that will not heal until Whites accept Blacks as equal citizens.

Whites in the state have grudgingly admitted the contributions of Black citizens to Kentucky culture in several areas but have also ignored Black contributions to the state in other areas, like popular music. In some sense, Blacks have become non-entities in Kentucky. They are there but not there. The popular thinking goes that Blacks have a separate but inferior culture with no overall meaning to Whites in Kentucky. Many Black citizens, in fact, have left the Commonwealth, disgusted with the state's lack of acceptance.

Such thinking by Whites produces various pernicious effects that affect Black citizens still living in the state. In many ways, it appears in the form of racism that elevates White culture and devalues Black culture. To some, Black culture is so different that, in their minds, it must be inferior—Black citizens being so different that they could not possibly contribute to the world of Whites, that they must not be relevant.

Conclusion

Until recently in the state, it was thought that an all-Black high school basketball team could not possibly win a state tournament. In fact, so the thinking went, Black athletes would always fail in their pursuits because of a lack of cognitive skills. High school basketball is extremely important to a great majority of Kentuckians. The Kentucky state high school basketball tournament has become an "appropriate" place for Whites to express their views on the "inferiority" of Black athletes specifically and Black people generally. It was believed that Black athletes would always prove their inferiority and never triumph.

Black students, until the last few years, went to separate schools, with the chance to go to Lincoln Institute, an all-Black boarding school, the only real chance for students to have exposure to a well-funded education. Of course, the Supreme Court supposedly put an end to the need for such a school, but traditionally Black schools are sorely lacking in state funding. This means that many Black students still lack good educations, and as a result, they often occupy only the meanest of jobs. Some Black students even drop out of school before their education is complete to face a lifetime of disappointing employment.

The recent Education Reform Act promised changes but quickly reverted to old, "more comfortable" ways, hiding the discrimination of White lawmakers and state officials. In Berry's terms, Black citizens have become a separate culture whose existence escapes the attention of Whites.

BIBLIOGRAPHY

Capps, Randall. *The Rowan Story: From Federal Hill to My Old Kentucky Home.* Cincinnati, OH: Creative Company, 1976.

Eldridge, Carrie. "1847: Kentucky Raid: The Underground Railroad and Fugitive Slave Law in Cass County, Michigan." December 2020. https://theclio.com/entry/entry/85110.

Everman, Henry. *Bourbon County Since 1865.* N.p., 1999.

Fee, John. *The Autobiography of John Fee.* Chicago: National Christian Association, 1892.

Fischer, Gerald. *Guerrilla Warfare in Kentucky.* Morley, MO: Acclaim Press, 2014.

Harrison, Lowell. *The Civil War in Kentucky.* Lexington: University Press of Kentucky, 1975.

Harrison, Lowell, and James Klotter. *A New History of Kentucky.* Lexington: University Press of Kentucky, 1997.

Kleber, John, ed. *The Kentucky Encyclopedia.* Lexington: University Press of Kentucky, 1992.

Klingaman, William. *Abraham Lincoln and the Road to Emancipation.* New York: Viking, 2001.

Klotter, James, et al. *Kentucky Profiles.* Frankfort: Kentucky Historical Society, 1982.

Lonn, Ella. *Desertion in the Civil War.* Lincoln: University of Nebraska Press, 1928.

Lucas, Marion. *A History of Blacks in Kentucky.* Lexington: University Press of Kentucky, 1992.

Marshall, Anne E. *Creating a Confederate Kentucky*. Chapel Hill: University of North Carolina Press, 2010.

Ramage, James. *Rebel Raider*. Lexington: University Press of Kentucky, 1986.

Schwemm, Robert C. "Strader vs. Graham: Kentucky's Contribution to National Slavery in Litigation and the Dred Scott Decision." *Kentucky Law Journal* 97, no. 3 (2008–9): 353–438.

Sears, Richard D. *Camp Nelson: A Civil War History*. Lexington: University Press of Kentucky, 2002.

Sehlinger, Peter J. *Kentucky's Last Cavalier*. Frankfort: Kentucky Historical Society, 2004.

Smith, Gerard, et al. *The Kentucky African American Encyclopedia*. Lexington: University Press of Kentucky, 2015.

Sutherland, Donald E. *American Civil War Guerrillas*. Santa Barbara, CA: Prager, 2013.

Tallant, Harold D. *Evil Necessity*. Lexington: University Press of Kentucky, 2003.

INDEX

B

Bramlette, Governor Thomas 11, 15, 82, 83, 84
Brown, John 44, 56, 57, 59
Burbridge, Stephen 14, 62, 78, 79, 80, 88, 89, 97, 100, 103
Burnam, Curtis 12, 41

C

Camp Nelson 14, 59, 89, 93, 95, 104
Cass County 44, 47, 48

D

Dred Scott decision 11, 16, 30, 31, 32, 35

E

"evil necessity" of slavery, the 10, 26

F

Ferguson, Champ 88
Fry, General Speed 96, 97
Fugitive Slave Law 12, 14, 46, 104

G

Graham Springs 32, 33
guerrilla warfare 9, 14, 15, 62, 78, 80, 88, 89, 90, 91, 92, 100

K

Keckley, Elizabeth 14, 73, 74, 75, 76, 77

L

Lee, General Robert E. 55, 56, 66, 91, 100, 101
Lincoln, Mary Todd 14, 73, 74, 75, 76, 77

M

Madison County 13, 37, 56, 58, 59, 81, 86
Magruder, Henry 88, 89
"My Old Kentucky Home" 67, 68, 69, 70, 71, 72

O

"Old Clothes Scandal" 75

P

Paris, Kentucky 47

S

Simpsonville Massacre 90
slavery 8, 9, 19, 24, 26, 30, 31, 32, 35, 36, 38, 44, 45, 47, 50, 55, 56, 58, 68, 79, 93, 99, 103
Strader v. Graham case 30, 32, 35, 36

T

Taney, Roger B. 31, 35, 36
Thirteenth Amendment 11, 12, 17, 37, 40, 41, 42, 43, 82, 83, 84, 95

U

U.S. Constitution 10, 11, 16, 27, 31, 37, 38, 39, 40, 42, 47, 94, 95, 101, 103

ABOUT THE AUTHOR

Dr. Marshall Myers is a retired rhetoric and literature professor at Eastern Kentucky University. He is president of the Madison County Civil War Roundtable and served on the Kentucky Civil War Sesquicentennial Commission. Myers is a member of the Kentucky Historical Society and the Madison County Historical Society. He has published more than 250 articles, poems, short stories and scholarly pieces. He earned his PhD at the University of Louisville.

Visit us at
www.historypress.com